The Saturday Book

Twenty-fourth Year

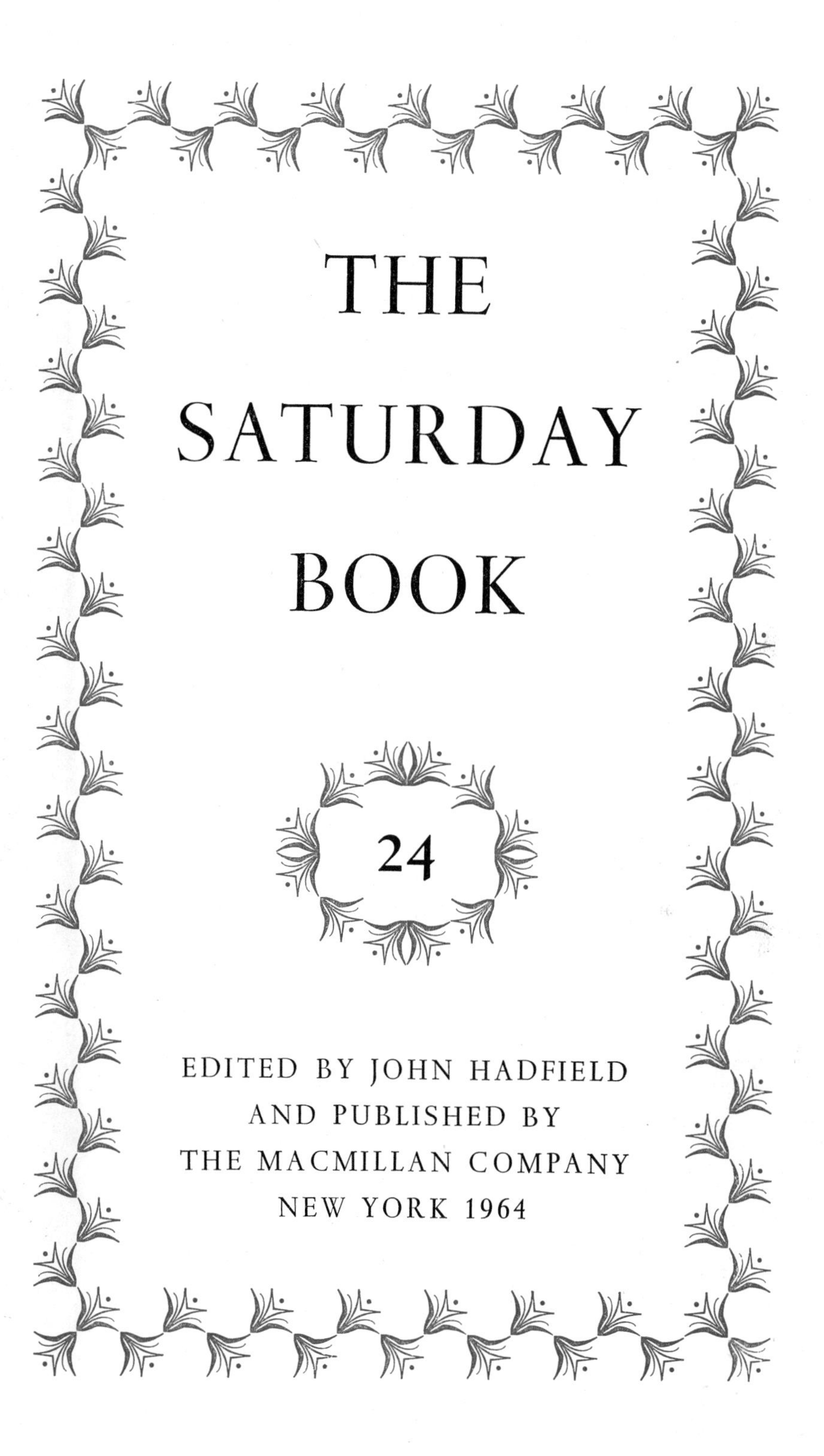

THE SATURDAY BOOK

24

EDITED BY JOHN HADFIELD
AND PUBLISHED BY
THE MACMILLAN COMPANY
NEW YORK 1964

Printed in Great Britain

First published in the United States
of America by the MacMillan
Company 1964

The frontispiece reproduces a Flower Piece by Rachel Ruysch (1664–1750) which is in the Rijksmuseum, Amsterdam.

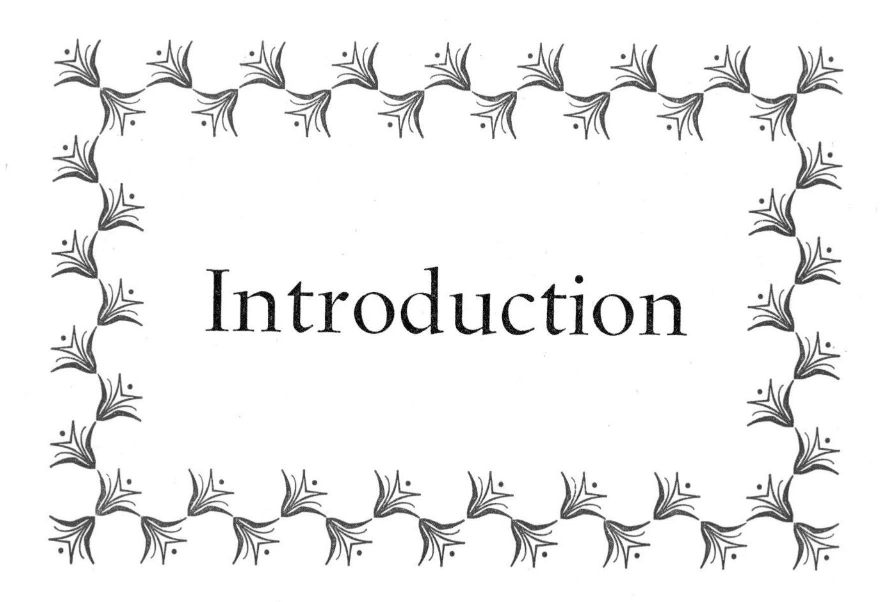

Introduction

Last year's issue of *The Saturday Book* was sold out three weeks before Christmas—not quite a record, but nearly. Why, we asked ourselves once again, does this curious rag-bag of a book continue to hold, and even extend, its public?

In his recent *Confessions of an Advertising Man* Mr David Ogilvy, the Englishman who made such a brilliant career in salesmanship in the United States, tells us that there are three magic words which sell things: 'free', 'darling', and 'new'. Out of idle curiosity we glanced back at the blurb and contents list of last year's *S.B.* to see if we had, without realizing it, employed any of these talismans of success.

There was no mention of anything being 'free'; indeed the price was all too conspicuously printed on the package. Nor, as far as casual perusal went, was there any use of the word 'darling'. The nearest to it was a reference to 'a perfect dear', which, you will agree, is rather a different thing. The opening feature of the book, however, was a long, impressive, illustrated survey of 'The NEW Jewellers'.

Needless to say, this fortuitous choice of the word NEW for one feature bore little relation to the contents of the book as a whole. There was a feature lamentably entitled 'Any OLD Iron?' There was another one on the year 1907—appallingly *vieux jeu*! And Beverley Nichols wrote about his Great-Great-Great-Aunt.

Nevertheless we must suppose that the single use of this magic word NEW in our opening feature had some effect in setting the cash-registers ringing.

Are you to suppose, Loyal Readers, that because of this lucky chance, you are going to find this and future issues of *The Saturday Book* stuffed with novelties, which will cause you to exclaim, with Browning,

How strange it seems, and new!

The actual context in which Browning used that line might be relevant to our aims. Nostalgia is only permissible when it revives the spirit. But we do not regard novelty, *per se*, as an absolute recommendation.

The official catalogue of the recent Gulbenkian International Exhibition of modern art put forward the curiously phrased proposition that valid works of the *avant-garde* should 'offend' the public by being 'genuinely unacceptable, despicable and disgusting'.

The *épatement* of the *bourgeoisie* is, of course, a traditional process of taste and fashion. Many great artists have had to pass through that phase. What seems apparent today is that a huge number of minor artists have become completely wrapped up, not in basic aesthetic problems, but in the incidental processes of 'disgusting' and 'offending'. Theirs is not an austere disregard of fashion but an over-eager concern with the (often highly profitable) gimmicks of anti-fashion.

We of *The Saturday Book* would not dream of making any important aesthetic claims for our miscellany. But on one point we take a modest but firm stand. We have no wish to 'offend' or to 'disgust'. We unashamedly prefer, if we can, to please.

You won't find anything specifically NEW in this issue. Nor, alas, can we pretend that it is FREE. But, DARLINGS, we love you!

J.H.

Contents

A LOOKING GLASS FOR LADIES

Women Painters: James Laver 10
Edwin Smith's Domestic Alphabet 26
Four Fearless Females: Madge Garland 57
The Girl in the Baker's: John Moore 72
Conversation Pieces of the 'Sixties: Eleanor Farjeon 75
Ladies in Love: Charles Gibbs-Smith 87
Shall We Dance?: John Pitt 109
Room-Mates: Mary Margaret Revell 121

LEAVES FROM A SKETCH BOOK

Malta Victorious: Laurence Scarfe 127

A MIRROR FOR MEN

Sandow, the Strong Man: Frank W. Lane 140
The World of Charles Hamilton: Robert Kelly 148
Fire! Fire!: Amoret and Christopher Scott 161
SF Art: Brian W. Aldiss 170
Get Your Hair Cut!: Olive Cook 185
The Old School Tie—and all that: Angus McGill 191
Lament for the Walking Stick: Margaret Aldred 199

A CABINET OF CURIOSITIES

Arcimboldo: Bernard Denvir 205
Citizen Train: Miriam Allen De Ford 218
Breakfast with Oscar: Beverley Nichols 229
Put it in Your Diary: Fred Bason 234

THE SATURDAY BOOK STORY

The Travellers: Anthony Glyn 241
With a drawing by Lynton Lamb

The verses from 'Romance' by W. J. Turner on page 245 are reprinted by permission of the Oxford University Press.

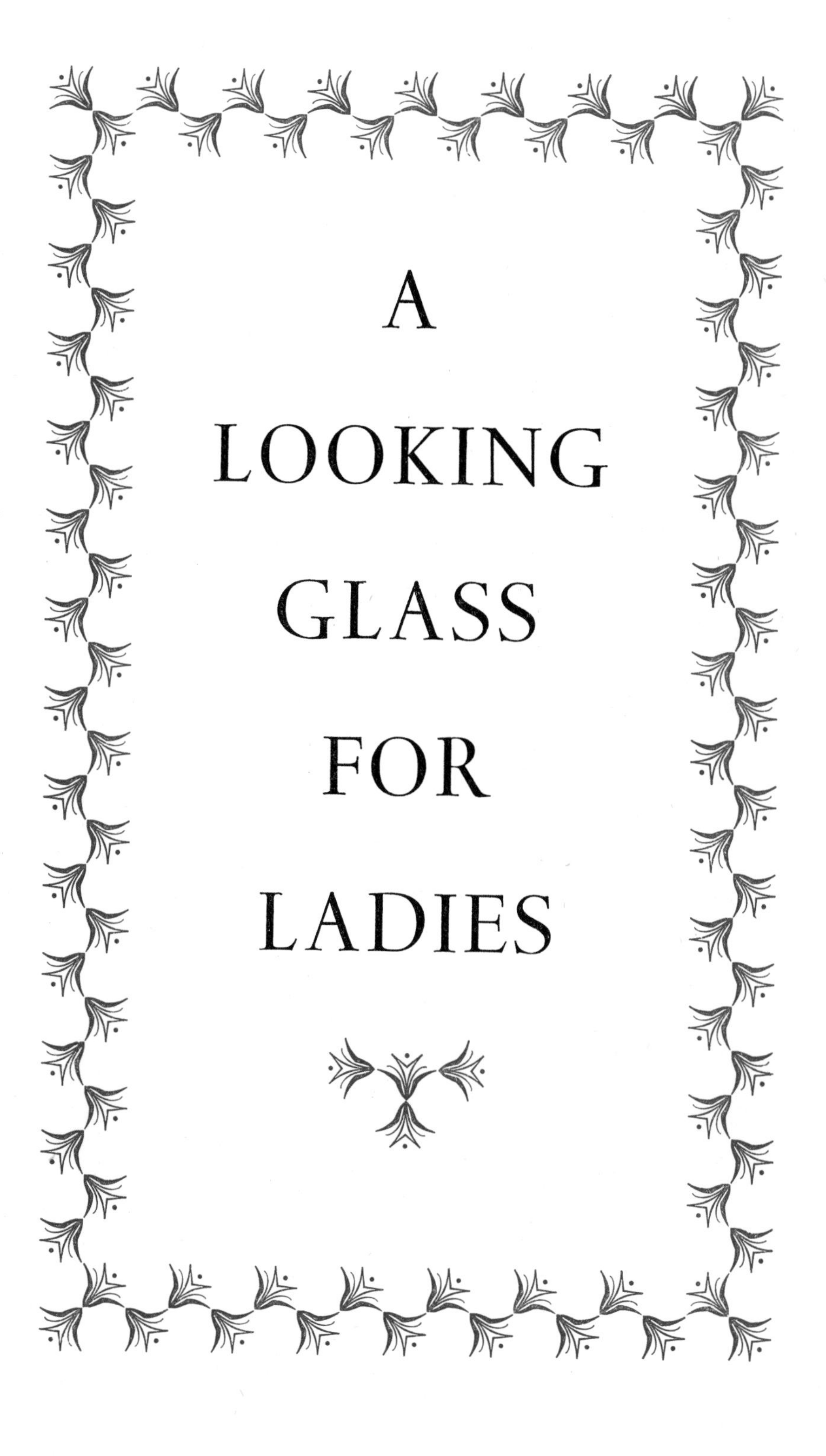

A LOOKING GLASS FOR LADIES

Women Painters

JAMES LAVER

WOMEN today seem to have taken up painting in a big way. There are tens of thousands of amateur artists in Britain and the United States, a large proportion of them women. But is the use of the phrase 'in a big way' quite apt? If it merely means that there are a lot of women painters, well and good; but if it implies that there is anything 'big' about the work they produce the suggestion is open to doubt. Have women *ever* painted 'in a big way'?

Women are universally agreed to be admirable exponents of the applied and interpretive arts—interior decoration, handicrafts, dancing, and acting. But in the creative arts have they ever reached the heights? Apart from the legendary Sappho, is there any supreme woman poet? And in painting is there any female Leonardo, Raphael, or Michelangelo? Perhaps not, but it is certainly not for want of trying.

Even the ancient Greeks had women painters whose names—but not, alas, their works—have come down to us: Aristarete, celebrated for her picture of Æsculapius, Anaxandra, and Helena, who painted the Battle of Issus in the fourth century B.C. Only one woman painter in ancient Rome is recorded, and she was a Greek, Lala by name, who painted miniatures in the first century B.C.

Nothing much more is heard of female artists until the late Middle Ages when a number of what Walter Shaw Sparrow calls 'gifted and gracious nuns' painted holy pictures in the style of Fra Angelico and Fra Bartolommeo. Most of the nuns were anonymous, but a recorded name is that of Plautilla Nelli who had gifts also of administration, for she became Prioress of the Convent of St Catherine in Florence. In Germany we hear of Sister Marguerita, a nun at Nuremberg, who worked from 1459 to 1470 and copied many religious works.

In the sixteenth century in Italy, at last, there was quite a burst of female talent, some of it good enough to reach professional

CONSTANCE MARIE CHARPENTIER

Portrait of Charlotte du Val d'Ognes

(Metropolitan Museum of Art, New York: Bequest of Isaac D. Fletcher)

ARTEMESIA GENTILESCHI
Self-portrait (Spencer Collection)

Below, on the left:

ANGELICA KAUFFMANN
Self-portrait (Galleria dell' Accademia di San Luca, Rome)

On the left:

ROSALBA CARRIERA
Portrait of a Young Woman
(Musée National
du Louvre,
Paris)

Above:

LOUISE VIGÉE LE BRUN
Portrait of Madame Grant
(Metropolitan Museum of
Art, New York. Bequest of
Edward S. Harkness, 1940)

SUZANNE VALADON: Maurice Utrillo and his Grandmother
(Musée d'Art Moderne, Paris)

status. The most notable woman painter of the period was Sophonisba Anguisciola, whose precocity was such that when little more than a child she painted a self-portrait and sent it to Pope Julius III. She was only twenty-six when she was summoned to the Spanish Court by Philip II, who was so pleased with her work that he showered her with favours, married her to a wealthy Sicilian noble, and himself provided the dowry of 12,000 ducats, an enormous sum at that period. Van Dyck met her in Genoa in 1622, when she was old and nearly blind, and he was enchanted by her conversation. She was certainly a most competent artist, and her painting of her three young sisters playing chess has great charm. Vasari said of this picture that 'the figures wanted only voice to be alive'.

Talented contemporaries were Artemesia Gentileschi, who painted both portraits and religious pictures in the style of Guido Reni and Domenichino; Lavinia Fontana, who made portraits of Pope Paul V and a whole line of cardinals; and Elizabeth Sirani, whose huge canvas of the Baptism of Christ was painted when she was little more than twenty. Women artists have often been accused by male rivals of not painting their own pictures. Elizabeth Sirani rebutted this slander by painting a portrait of Leopold of Tuscany 'before an audience of distinguished persons'; a hard test, one would have thought, for any portrait painter.

In the eighteenth century the most famous woman artist in Italy was the portraitist Rosalba Carriera. She was born in Venice in 1675 and began her artistic career as a designer of point-de-Venise lace, but when towards the end of the century the demand for this was very much reduced she turned her attention to the decoration of snuff-boxes. She also attempted painting in oil, but soon began to specialize in the pastel portrait. Pastel is a medium suited (to put it bluntly) to those who cannot draw with absolute precision. A lively feeling for colour harmony, and the decorative sense which women often possess, concealed the weakness of her draughtsmanship, and her crayon portraits soon found eager purchasers. At the age of thirty she was elected a member of the Academy of St Luke at Rome, and this was a great honour for a woman artist. She was so highly regarded in other parts of Italy that Cosimo III, Grand Duke of Tuscany, asked her to contribute a self-portrait to the Uffizi, where it can still be seen. Her fame spread to France and during the year (1720) which she spent in Paris she depicted King Louis XV, then a boy of ten, and many notables of the Court. Returning to Venice, she continued her successful career until her sight failed ten years before her death in 1757. The many pastels which have survived give, unfortunately, a very poor notion of the effect they must have produced when they were new. The tints have faded and, as pastel is a dry powder, any shock to the surface to which it is applied tends to shake it off. It requires a fixative of some kind and this inevitably detracts from the brilliance of the original work.

It would be strange if the great surge of artistic activity in the Netherlands in the seventeenth century had not thrown up some women painters. Long before that Marguerite, sister of the brothers Van Eyck, had made a name for herself in art, although almost nothing survives which can be attributed to her with any certainty. A century later we find the interesting figure of Suzanne Honthorst. Her father, Gerard Honthorst, came from Ghent to England and was received with favour by King Henry VIII. The King admired the daughter's work also, and she made a rich marriage with John Parker, one of the King's archers.

In the seventeenth century in Holland there was a great fashion for flower paintings, and one would expect women to excel in this genre. Indeed one finds a whole list of names: Catherine Peeters, Marie Baesten, and, most attractive of all, Rachel Ruysch. Some women artists tried to emulate Frans Hals, but the vigorous brush-strokes of the master were beyond their capability. One has only to look at the works of a painter like Judith Leyster to detect the weakness of the feminine hand.

France was one of the first countries to give women painters official recognition. The Académie Royale de Peinture et de Sculpture, founded in 1666, opened its doors to women from the beginning, and during the next hundred years fifteen were admitted. Nearly all these belonged to one or other of the 'painting families'. They were the wives, the daughters, the sisters, or the nieces of artists, and we find among them such well-known names as Natoire, Perrocel, and Van Loo. Madame Vigée Le Brun was the wife of the picture dealer Le Brun and the daughter of a portrait painter. She was received into the Académie on May 31, 1783, on the same day as her great rival Madame Adélaide Labille Guyard. The latter had, perhaps, the more solid talent, but Madame Vigée Le Brun's canvases, especially those depicting herself and her young daughter, have a considerable, if somewhat sentimental, charm.

In a rather different category are those women artists who 'assisted' their husbands or lovers, and in their own work the influence of the master shows through very plainly. Marguerite Gérard is a reflection of Fragonard, and Mlle Ledoux of Greuze; and Constance Mayer, whose unhappy love affair with Prudhon ended in suicide, painted in exactly the same style.

Occasionally we find the works of a pupil or disciple mistaken for those of the master, and there could scarcely be a higher compliment, even if subsequent research proves the attribution to have been mistaken. An interesting case is a painting now in the Metropolitan Museum, New York. It is a portrait of Charlotte du Val d'Ognes, who is said to have been a pupil of David, and the picture was long attributed to the great French classicist. David, however, himself compiled a catalogue of his works and this is not mentioned among them. Also, although the painting is extremely attractive as a period piece, there are certain weaknesses of which a painter of David's calibre would hardly have been guilty. The back is excessively long, the limbs are somewhat awkwardly drawn, and the folds of the draperies conventional. The complex effects of reflected light and the background enlivened with figures are more typical of Gérard than of David. The picture must therefore have been painted by someone who was influenced by both.

The choice of the art experts has fallen on Constance Marie Charpentier, for in the museum at Amiens there is a painting entitled 'Melancholy' which is known to be by her and which is stylistically very similar. She was born in 1767 and exhibited at the Paris salons between 1795 and 1819, and in the Salon of 1801 she showed 'Melancholy' and other pictures. A contemporary critic praises one of these as 'a very remarkable portrait of a young woman almost entirely in shadow, this difficult effect of light being well felt, the shadows grey, and the general tonality cold'. We may therefore conclude, in the words of the Metropolitan Museum catalogue, that 'the old attribution of our portrait to David is definitely refuted and that its ascription to Mme Charpentier has a strong probability'.

In England the first woman artist of any note was Mary Beale, the daughter of a Suffolk clergyman, who lived between the years 1632 and 1697. She modelled her style on that of Lely and was patronized by King Charles II and other distinguished persons, in spite of the fact, as contemporary chronicles tell us, that 'she never hesitated to tell the truth'. Her portrait of the poet Abraham Cowley, now in the National Portrait Gallery, shows both psychological penetration and great technical skill.

Lady Diana Beauclerk was a talented amateur whose compositions, in spite of the weakness of the drawing, are not without charm. Angelica Kauffmann was more professional, and her work was admired by two such different persons as Goethe and Sir Joshua Reynolds. She was a Swiss by birth, but came to England in 1765, and three years later, on the foundation of the Royal Academy, she was nominated as one of the original thirty-six members. She contributed no less than eighty-two pictures to the annual exhibitions between 1769 and 1797.

Unfortunately for her happiness the sentimentality of her pictures spilled over into her private life. She allowed herself to be trapped into a clandestine marriage with the valet of the Swedish Count de Horn who passed himself off as his master. Having got rid of this man by a payment of £300, she next married the Venetian painter Antonio Zucchi and retired with him to Rome. Her pictures are in most of the European galleries and she herself was twice painted by Sir Joshua Reynolds.

A contemporary of Angelica Kauffmann was Catherine Read. Her work is surprisingly free from sentimentality even when she was painting children. Little is known of her life, but she sent frequently to the exhibitions in what has been called 'the Reynolds period'. She specialized in female portraits, many of which were reproduced in mezzotint and were much admired.

In the nineteenth century women artists seem to fall behind a little. There is no female Turner, no female Constable, no great name at all. Water-colour painting was now considered a desirable accomplishment for all young ladies; it was included in the curriculum of 'Ladies' Academies', together with the pianoforte and 'the use of the globes'. But the results are not very impressive. Few women seem to have attempted oil painting, either as amateurs or professionals. Two figures, however, stand out: in France the formidable Rosa Bonheur, and in England Lady Elizabeth Butler.

Rosa Bonheur was the daughter of a drawing master and showed precocious talent. Her father tried to force her into the business of dressmaking but finally relented and taught her himself. Her first picture was exhibited at the Salon when she was eighteen, and in 1845, when she was only twenty-three, she had no less than fourteen pictures in the annual exhibition. Her best-known painting, 'The Horse Fair', was shown in 1853 and was sold at a very high figure. Rosa now adopted male attire, which she only abandoned when she went to receive the Cross of the Legion of Honour at the hands of the Empress Eugénie.

Lady Elizabeth Butler specialized in battle pieces such as 'The Thin Red Line' and 'Steady the Drums and Fifes'. These were painted with considerable vigour and an attention to the details of military uniform which rendered them very popular, especially in the form of photogravure reproductions.

The passion for 'costume pieces' was equally prevalent in France, and the Salon contained year by year examples by such women painters as Jeanne Rongier and Mlle Achille-Fould. For the most part they were weak in drawing and lamentably ignorant of historical costume. But, side by side with these Salon exhibitors, there was a small group of women painters owing their allegiance to the new Impressionist school.

One of the most talented of these was Berthe Morisot. There was a long artistic tradition in her family, for she was the great-grand-daughter of Fragonard. She was born at Bourges in 1841, studied painting under good masters, and was much encouraged by the advice and help of Père Corot. In 1865 she met Manet; she worked in his studio, served him as model, and, in 1874, married his younger brother Eugéne. Manet painted her portrait several times and she appears with others in some of his most important pictures like 'Le Balcon'. After the middle 'eighties, however, Manet's influence waned, for she fell under the influence of Renoir and Monet. She was never merely derivative but was a good and original painter in her own right. The light palette of the Impressionists suited her femininity better than the rather sombre tones of Manet, and some of her later pictures positively glow with light. She died in Paris in 1895.

Another woman painter influenced by the Impressionists was Mary Cassat. Although born in America, she was of French education as her childhood was spent in Paris. After studying at Philadelphia and in Italy, Spain, and Belgium, she settled definitely in the French capital in 1879 and was invited by Degas to join the Impressionist group. He was a great admirer of her work and is said to have exclaimed, on seeing one of her drawings: 'I can't admit that any woman should draw as well as that!' She excelled in her studies of children, painted without sentimentality but with singular charm.

The background of both Berthe Morisot and Mary Cassat was comfortably middle class. Very different was the extraordinary career of Suzanne Valadon. Born at Limoges in 1867, she came to Paris as a child and performed as an acrobat in a circus. Falling from a trapeze and sustaining injuries which made it impossible for her to appear again, she obtained work as an artist's model. She posed for Puvis de Chavannes, Renoir, and other famous painters and began to realize that she had some artistic talent herself. Toulouse-Lautrec, who lived near her lodgings in Montmartre, introduced her to dealers, and her drawings of nudes began to find a market. She travelled about France and as far as Corsica, painting landscapes, still life, and flowers. She was a considerable artist in her own right, but she is now chiefly remembered as the mother of Utrillo.

Marie Bashkirtseff falls into another category again, for her work was hardly touched by the innovations of the Impressionists. Born near Poltawa in 1860, she was brought to Paris as a child and at first studied to be a singer. While still very young she entered the Académie Julian, which by this time—the late 'seventies—had somewhat lost its reputation. She was much influenced by the 'realist' work of Bastien-Lepage and produced several pictures in his manner. Her self-portrait, which was produced for the Luxembourg, is a penetrating study of a young woman tormented by ill-health and all the conflicting pressures of the Slav temperament. Hers was a sad life. She became ill in 1878, at the very threshold of her career, and by 1884 she was dead. She is now chiefly remembered for her diary, published in 1887, perhaps one of the most heart-revealing records ever penned.

Unfortunately there was no woman artist in England in the second half of the nineteenth century who could compare in any way with Berthe Morisot and Suzanne Valadon. Most of them were but the pale reflections of their male contemporaries. There is a certain charm in Mrs William De Morgan's imitations of Burne-Jones, and in the diluted Watts of Mrs Anna Lea Merritt. The latter's 'Love Locked Out' was purchased for the Chantrey Collection and was enormously popular in photogravure reproductions. Equally popular was Margaret Isabel Dicksee's picture of 'The Child Handel' and Lady Alma-Tadema's 'Nothing Venture, Nothing Have', a study of children dressed in a not very convincing version of seventeenth-century costume.

Kate Greenaway was chiefly an illustrator and would hardly be included in the present survey if Ruskin, in one of the strangest aberrations of the critical mind, had not compared her (rather to her advantage) with Michelangelo. Two noble ladies made something of a mark as amateurs: Louisa, Marchioness of Waterford, and the Marchioness of Granby. The latter's pencil portraits of men like Lord Salisbury and Cecil Rhodes are not without merit; the former's more ambitious efforts, especially her religious paintings like 'Jesus Christ among the Doctors', merely display the inadequacy of her colour and draughtsmanship. Mrs Helen Allingham painted some attractive, if sentimental, landscapes, somewhat marred by the greenery-yallery colour scheme to which she remained faithful all her life.

For one of the most original women painters of the twentieth century we have to go back to France, to Marie Laurencin (the subject of an essay in last year's *Saturday Book*). She was born in

Paris in 1885, and by 1907 was exhibiting at the Salon d'Automne. Her early paintings were sombre in tone and rather in the manner of Carrière, but immediately after the First World War she blossomed into a style of her own, a style essentially feminine, with its rose-pink, apple-green, and sky-blue tints. Her subjects were mostly young girls, painted in flat tones, with the features simplified and the noses sometimes omitted altogether. Some of her paintings tremble on the edge of 'chocolate-box' prettiness, but at her best she sounded a note of striking originality. She was also an etcher and engraver of considerable merit. She was one of the very few women painters in the history of art whose work cannot be seen as a reflection of some male master, and whose pictures could only have been painted by a woman.

It would be impossible in this brief survey to do justice to the women painters of the present century, though mention should be made of two highly idiosyncratic artists of our time, one English, one American. Gwen John, sister of Augustus John, specialized in rather wry, sad paintings of girls and young women; Grandma Moses, a genuine naive, depicted American farm scenes with singular charm.

As art schools multiplied, girl students flocked to them, but many found scope for their talents, not as painters, but as designers. 'Good taste' is not usually an attribute of the greatest painters; in fact, as Degas remarked to Whistler, it can be a positive danger. The great artist finds his subjects everywhere; he does not need to arrange the flowers 'artistically' or have the dress laundered before he sets to work. It is probably the 'good taste' of women artists which prevents them from reaching the heights. So, women painters, when they are not merely echoing the works of some chosen master (often a master with whom they have some emotional relationship), tend to excel in the minor arts. None the less, the list of women artists we have been considering is impressive enough. The world would certainly be the poorer if brush and palette had never tempted them to try their hand.

BERTHE MORISOT: Le Berceau
(Louvre, Musée d'Impressionisme, Paris)

GWEN JOHN: Nude (Tate Gallery, London)

[24]

[25] ANNA LEA MERRITT. Love Locked Out (Tate Gallery, London)

EDWIN SMITH'S Domestic Alphabet

Adam style:
the library at
Kenwood House
Antimacassar
Apron
Attic:
at Croft Castle,
Herefordshire

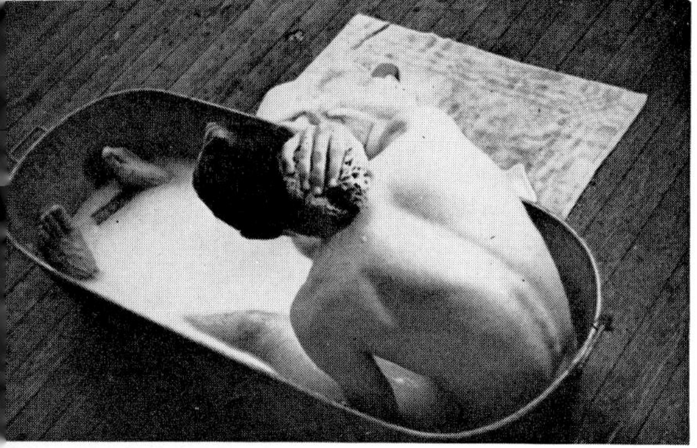

Bath
Bedroom
Bell-pull: at Russborough,
  Co. Wicklow
Bull's eye
Bungalow: the porter's lodge
  of the Great Hospital,
  Norwich

Caravan
Cast-iron curb
Chair: English, first quarter of the seventeenth century (V. & A. Museum)
Commode: in the Hotel D'Hane-Steenhuyse, Ghent

Door-case:
the Clifford's Inn Room, 1730
(V. & A. Museum)
Dormer window
Double front:
Woburn,
Bedfordshire

Egg and Dart moulding: in the Palazzo del Te (1524), Mantua, Italy
Egyptian House: Penzance, Cornwall
Electric light

Farm: The Furlongs, Glynde, Sussex
Fire-dogs
Floor: Welsh slate
Flower arrangement

Gables: Clare, Suffolk
Garden House:
The Grove,
Hampstead
Garden: Mitcham, Surrey
Gate: Bosham, Sussex
Grate: in the dining-room,
Arbury Hall,
Warwickshire

Half-timber:
Poynton Green,
Shropshire

Kitchen: Mr Tyler's bachelor flat, Poplar, E. Knocker

Inlay: Ballroom of the Hotel D'Hane-Steenhuyse, Ghent
Ironwork

Jacobean: Court cupboard, 1610 (V. & A. Museum)
Junk: Newcastle

Lamp
Lamp-post: at Berrington Hall, Herefordshire
Larder
Library: at Longleat House, Wiltshire

Leaded lights: Gifford's Hall, Stoke-by-Nayland
Lock: Blenheim Palace
Long Gallery: Knole House, Kent

Mangle: South Shields, Co. Durham
Mantelpiece: The Place, Bardfield, Essex
Marquetry: a 'Tunbridge ware' box (V. & A. Museum

Mask: the hall fireplace,
Caerhays Castle, Cornwall
Mathematical tiles:
Lewes, Sussex
Mirror
Muddle

Name: Fitzjohn's Avenue, London, N.W.3
Newel: the staircase, Knole House, Kent
Notice: in Wilton House, Salisbury

Occasional table: in Croft Castle
Oriel: Blakeney, Norfolk
Oriental: Boundary Road, St John's Wood
Overmantel: English, 1770 (V. & A. Museum)

Pebbles: Morston, Norfolk
Perambulator: New York, c. 1900
Pier Glass
Plant (Mrs Tom Wheeler, Broadhaven, Pembs.)

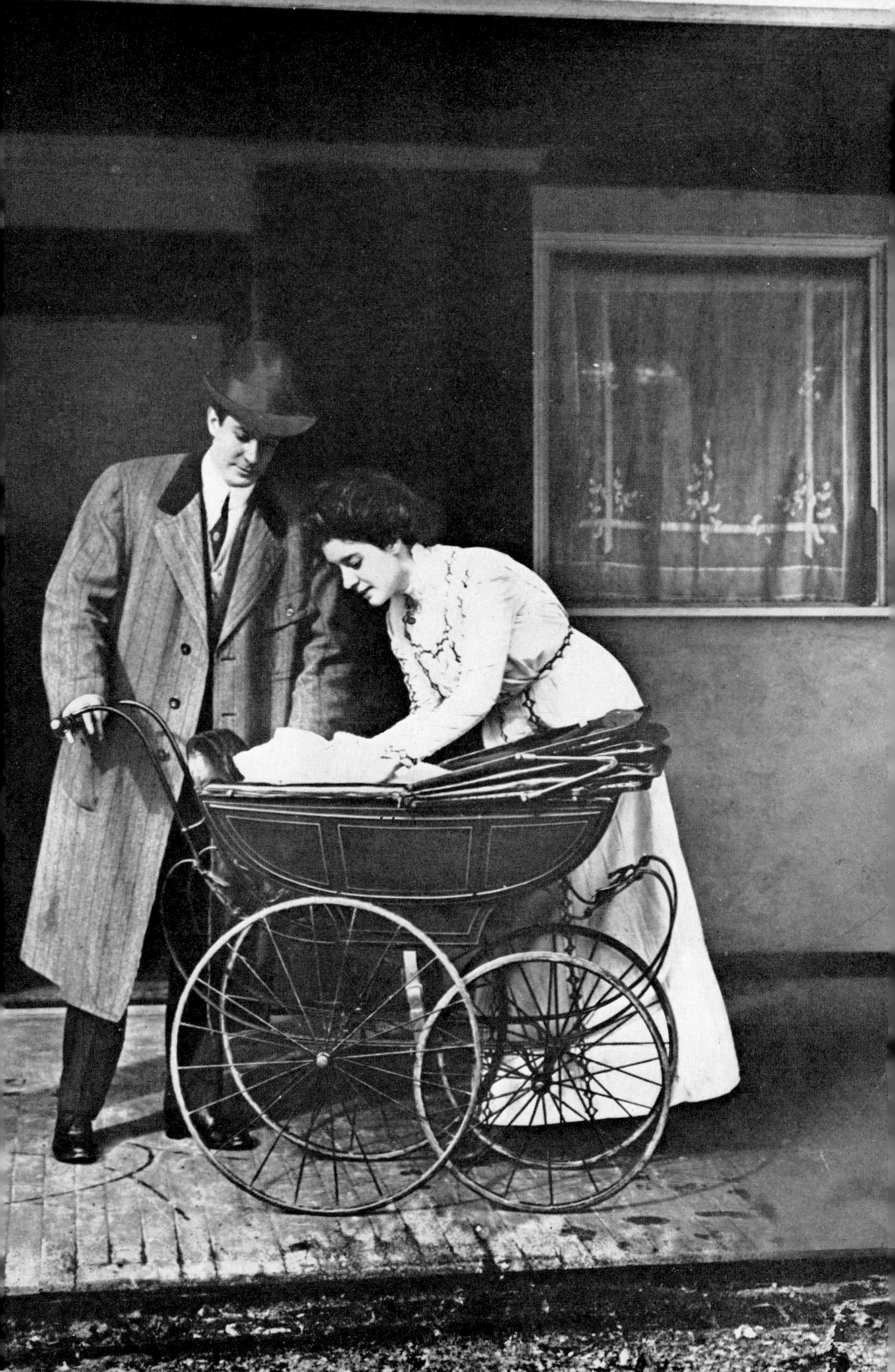
2585

Rustication: the Petit Château de Tanlay, France, 1640
Rug: Stoddart's Carpet Museum, Paisley
Rustic chair: English mid-eighteenth century (V. & A. Museum)

Semi-detached:
near Eyeworth, Beds.
Settee: a Tutankhamen
replica (Miss Marie Gray)

Shingles: Southwold, Suffolk
Skin rug
Slates: St Columb Major, Cornwall
Statuary: Clopton House, Warwickshire

PEACE

Tapestry: a bedroom at Knole House, Kent
Telephone: Egeskov Castle, Denmark
Text
Topiary: Sapperton, Gloucestershire
Tradesman
Trellis
Turret: Craigievar Castle, Aberdeenshire

Verandah: College Crescent,
London, N.W.3

Washing: College Place,
London, N.W.1
W.C.: Croft Castle,
Herefordshire
Whitewash: Arncliffe,
Yorkshire
Wicker-work
Wooing

5

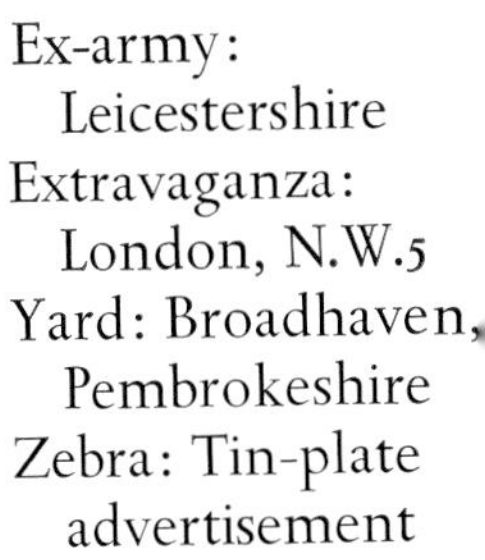

Ex-army: Leicestershire
Extravaganza: London, N.W.5
Yard: Broadhaven, Pembrokeshire
Zebra: Tin-plate advertisement

ALEXANDRINE PIETERNELLA FRANÇOISE TINNE

By Henry Comte de Montpézat. (Municipal Museum, The Hague)

Four Fearless Females

MADGE GARLAND

THE COURAGE most often associated with women is that of endurance rather than enterprise. If Miss Tully's reasoned calm surprises us less than Alexine Tinne's romantic bravery it is because the nineteenth century built up a picture of the ideal woman as submissive and home-loving, and as far as possible wished to ignore other aspects of her character. But during the last two centuries what a number of adventurous women there have been! And what difficulties they must have overcome even before they set out on their chosen roads—difficulties unimaginable to their emancipated descendants accustomed to packaged world tours.

Among the many less famous these four travellers each illustrate a different facet of bravery: Miss Tully, endurance; Alexine Tinne, visionary courage; Isabella Bird, unshakable self-possession; Daisy Bates, a splendid, lonely sacrifice for a lost cause.

It was no desire for adventure which led Miss Tully abroad, but merely family duty. Her brother, Richard Tully, was appointed first English consul to the Court of the Bashaw of Tripoli, and it was to accompany him and his family that she sailed for the shores of Libya in 1783.

Tripoli was then a walled town of cube-shaped buildings lime-washed to a glittering whiteness, its skyline broken by the domes of mosques and the green fronds of palm trees. Miss Tully wrote: 'The sea washes this town on three sides; and on the fourth it is divided from Egypt by dreary deserts . . . where none reside except occasionally the wandering Arab.' It is much the same today, except that to the desert's inhabitants one must now add the oil prospector, and several fine new buildings have been added beyond the walls. But as the traveller comes from the harbour into the city the first monument he sees is the arch of Marcus Aurelius which struck Miss Tully as 'one of the grandest arches of antiquity . . . thought by all good judges to be handsomer than any of the most celebrated in Italy'.

The consul's house was near the great battlemented castle, and his children, born and brought up in Tripoli and speaking Arabic, became the play-fellows of the Bashaw's numerous progeny. Miss Tully was freely admitted to the intimacy of the royal family, and her letters home are not only excellent examples of the Englishwoman's calm acceptance of extraordinary conditions abroad, but unique pictures of an African despot's private life at a time when it was virtually impossible for a Christian to enter the home of a Moor.

The appalling events which occurred during her ten years' visit do not appear to have disturbed her unduly, though she warns her correspondents that she will record 'such scenes and events . . . such sketches of human weakness and vice . . . effects of ambition, avarice, envy and intrigue as will seem scarcely credible' . . . for

> events which appear to us of such enormity, take place here without hesitation or inquiry. The head of a house whether father, brother or husband, having the power of life and death relative to the female part of his family, has only to get a teskerar of the Bashaw, which is a small bit of paper with his signature, giving leave to the person who requires it, to put to death the object of his anger; and this fatal paper is procured with the greatest facility.

Intrigue and murder were part of the daily round; slaves were bought, sold, and murdered with frequency and indifference; even the Circassians and Greeks, with whom most of the royal family were allied (for they could not marry a subject), might fall from power and security at the death of their master. Miss Tully recounts with phlegm the incident of a young widow who

> remained friendless and alone with two small children, deprived of all attendance and without the means of procuring necessaries for herself and infants . . . turned out of her house . . . [who] did not long survive her lamented lord . . . she was very beautiful with black eyes and brown hair and only fourteen years old when purchased and not more than twenty-nine when she died.

Such stories were common.

The measures taken to safeguard the women of the royal household were extraordinary. They were rarely allowed out and were then not only heavily veiled but surrounded by armed guards. In order to reach the harem in the castle it was necessary to traverse a number of vaulted underground passages which were so extremely dark and winding that Miss Tully had great difficulty in following her eunuch guide. The great iron door was guarded by armed eunuchs, and

inside a striking gloom prevails. The courtyard is grated over the top with heavy iron bars, very close together, giving it a melancholy appearance. The galleries round the courtyard are enclosed with lattices cut very small in wood . . . and the great number of attendants filling up every avenue makes it almost impossible to proceed from one apartment to another.

Yet in spite of such precautions innumerable intrigues flourished, secret notes were carried by the African slaves . . . 'the common instruments of mischief in the castle . . . and more than once machinations of a slave . . . ended in the death of her mistress'. Miss Tully recounts such highly coloured stories as that of glimpsing a mysterious veiled figure, believed to be a man, daring death in order to catch sight of the beloved, or of a grandson secretly soliciting an interview with his uncle's bride, whereupon the uncle, alerted, determined on the death of the nephew, but the latter 'managed to escape to the Bey's wife's apartments where he found asylum, lay concealed in a large chest in her room and during the night escaped to the country house of his mother'.

Miss Tully's measured prose shows no sign of panic when a serious famine overwhelmed the country, once called by the Romans the Granary of the World, but she regretted 'it is become horrid to walk or ride out, on account of the starved objects that continually die in the streets'.

Inevitably the famine was followed by plague, and the letters home described scenes of incredible horror. Three thousand persons died during the first two months: the

moment a death happens in a family, the alarm is given by the shrill screaming of the words 'wooliah-woo', repeated incessantly . . . these cries bring every female acquainted with or dependant on the family to scream over the dead . . . they likewise hire a number of women who make this horrid noise round the bier . . . and the women scratch their faces to such a degree that they appear to have been bled with a lancet.

During this time the Tullys maintained strict quarantine and remained shut up in their house for no less than thirteen months, while the corpses piled up in the streets outside.

After the plague 'the city exhibited an appearance awfully striking. In some of the houses were found the last victims that perished in them, who having died alone, unpitied and unassisted, lay in a state too bad to be removed from the spot . . . while in others, children were wandering about deserted.' The town was almost entirely depopulated, but among the survivors were some who acknowledged the compassion and attention shown them by the English consul and 'came forward to thank him with wild expressions of joy, calling him Boui [father] . . . they swear a faithful attachment to him, which there is no doubt they will show, in their way, as long as he is in the country'.

Fresh disasters befell the wretched city: the small amount of grain left was threatened by locusts from the Egyptian deserts, pirates entered the harbour after murdering all the passengers and sailors of a Venetian ship, another vessel took refuge in the bay with the plague on board and a return of the pestilence was feared. Civil war broke out between the Moors and Arabs and as the best troops were called away to fight the hostile tribesmen the city was left in a defenceless state. The consul and his family must have been glad of the protection promised them by the citizens in return for their generous behaviour during the plague.

Miss Tully writes that 'repeated descriptions of frequent skirmishes . . . near us . . . are so common, that I shall mention them only when they present any account . . . which I think may be new to you', and continues to fill her pages with detailed descriptions of the fantastic clothes worn by both men and women which never failed to delight her, and of some grandiose weddings which took place in the castle.

But, alas, political difficulties without were equalled by family dramas within, and the rivalries of the Bashaw's three sons culminated in one murdering another before his mother's eyes. Even so, the distracted father forgave his much-loved Benjamin, but was himself soon afterwards deposed and exiled by a Georgian adventurer who insisted that the European consuls should approach him barefooted. Famine, pestilence, and war were one matter, this was another, and the consul resigned. It must have been with relief that after ten years among such a wild people Miss Tully returned to England.

Rather more than half a century later another woman of exceptional courage, but of a very different calibre, visited Tripoli. No contrast could be greater than the rational, eighteenth-century Miss Tully and the romantic nineteenth-century Miss Tinne, dreaming of distant lands and mysterious people.

Alexandrine Pieternella Françoise Tinne, usually called Alexine, was born in 1835 to a Dutch Protestant family who lived in The Hague but had many English connections. When she was young she inherited a great fortune and was perhaps more indulged than most girls of her generation, but she was also unusually intelligent and early developed that interest in travel and 'scientific research' which was to lead to her tragic death.

It was sickness which first sent her abroad. She was spending the winter in Trieste with her mother and aunt when one of the party fell ill; the doctor prescribed sunshine, Egypt offered the most likely escape from the European climate, and when they arrived in Cairo they liked it so much that Alexine persuaded her relatives to settle there.

It was the day of the great explorers: Livingstone, Speke, Grant, and Baker were all alive, and their exploits were followed with breathless interest all over the world. Alexine soon decided she would like to make an expedition up the Nile. Accompanied by her mother, aunt, and two personal maids, she made her first adventurous journey. Rumours that she had been disappointed in love were current to explain such an unusual way of life for a beautiful young girl, but she always averred that she never wanted to marry, and in a letter to her nephew in England she once remarked that her greatest wish had always been to know what lay in the blank spot in the centre of the African continent.

The three ladies and their party ascended the Nile into the Sudan, reaching Gondokoro, then little more than a trading station for ivory-hunters and slave-traders. An eye-witness of the time described it as 'a veritable hell, a colony of cut-throats and drunken fellows—with nights made hideous by the snorting of hippos and the whistle of bullets'. It was also infested by mosquitoes and flies, but it boasted an Austrian mission church founded some ten years previously, and the Dutch ladies found the natives surprisingly clean.

Miss Tinne's money permitted her to travel in state, and she became known as 'Bent el Re' (King's daughter); she even managed to accommodate a grand piano on her *dahabiyah*, and the strains of Chopin could be heard echoing incongruously over the desert.

Madame Tinne was as fearless as her daughter. Alexine had given her mother a white donkey equipped with a comfortable padded back-rest and a parasol, and as the little beast was quicker than the other animals Madame Tinne was always the first to enter a strange village, where her unique equipage inevitably caused a tremendous sensation. Both mother and daughter were keen botanists, and after their death *Plantae Tinnaen*, a compendium of their joint botanical discoveries, was published in Vienna by their family.

In 1863 Alexine organized a great expedition to explore the region of the Bahr-al-Ghazal in the hope of discovering a great lake reputed to be in the heart of Africa, and also to look for Speke and Grant, who had been lost in the interior for over two years. In a large flotilla of boats the Dutch ladies, together with two German scientists, again ascended the Nile, but unfortunately illness overcame the party. They had to retire downstream to Khartoum and when Speke eventually appeared he was greeted not by Miss Tinne but by an equally lovely lady-traveller, the blonde Hungarian wife of Samuel Baker.

The doctor of the Dutch party was the first to succumb, and shortly afterwards Madame Tinne died, presumably of the blackwater fever which soon carried off the aunt and the two maids. Miss Tinne, although she complained bitterly at being left without a personal maid, continued her expedition alone.

On her return from Egypt she instructed her brother in England to buy her a steam yacht, and in this the 'Contesse

Olondese', as some called her, visited Algeria, Tunisia, and Tripoli. She was everywhere loved for her generosity and her good works. She nursed the sick when an epidemic broke out after an earthquake in Algiers, bought and freed slaves, paid highly for the services of her guides and dragomen, and sent splendid presents to the chiefs through whose territory she passed. Therefore there seemed no reason for the horrible disaster which befell her—but perhaps she had some premonition, for in her last letter to her nephew she spoke of death.

She planned another expedition to search for the legendary lake, now known as Lake Chad, but unmapped until the great Citroën expedition of 1922. She set out from the same Tripoli where in the previous century Miss Tully had written her letters, intending to reach the centre of Africa by a south-easterly route across the Sahara. This would take her through the country of the mysterious veiled men, the Tuaregs. She was warned of the unreliability of the tribe but could not be persuaded to change her mind. She set off towards Ghat, a Turkish fort on the frontiers of the Fezzan not far from the Tassili massif, where explorers of this century have discovered some of the world's most sensational prehistoric wall-paintings. The water required for the arduous crossing of the Sahara was contained in great iron tanks carried on pack animals, and their shape, together with Alexine's munificence, gave rise to the rumour that they were the treasure-chests of this wonderful princess.

Although she had not omitted to send gifts to the local chiefs and had rewarded her Tuareg guides handsomely, they and her camel-drivers conspired to murder her and seize what they thought was her hoard of gold. One day when encamped at a lonely well in the desert she heard an argument, went to the door of her tent, and raised her hand to command silence. This was the signal. Her attackers fell on her. The first spear-thrust missed her body and half severed one of her hands, which she ineffectually tried to set back on her wrist; the second nearly cut her head from her body and her long plait fell down. She was then stripped of her clothes and dragged out from the tent and left in the burning sun. Her faithful woman Saadah, a negro slave whom she had bought and liberated but who would never leave her, tried to go to her, but was torn away, and the poor woman remained conscious for hours, calling weakly for water. The two Dutch sailors from the yacht who had accompanied her were also murdered.

This frightful event caused a great sensation, and the world's newspapers carried accounts of 'this charming Diana, mistress of many tongues', whose work was so unusual and whose end so atrocious. She was only thirty-four when she died, and for a long time her memory lingered on in the wild districts she had visited, as a legendary demi-goddess, rich, beautiful, and kind.

No one could be less like the tall, blonde Alexine than Isabella Bird, who was five feet in height, and preferred mundane facts to legendary lakes. Only in courage were they equal and—once again—it was ill-health which sent the traveller on her way.

Isabella Bird was in her early twenties when her doctor, bewildered by her symptoms, suggested a sea-voyage might do her good. She had had a serious operation on her spine, and occasionally brief mentions of this weakness occur in her travel diaries; but her trouble seems to have been alleviated rather than aggravated by the hardships she endured. Today she would be known as a schizophrenic; then she was merely called a 'lady-traveller'. No one appeared to consider it strange that when comfortably at home she 'suffered from spinal prostration and could seldom rise before noon . . . wrote propped up on a pillow, a flat writing-board on her knees . . . and only sacrificed an hour or so to privileged visitors', yet once abroad she could climb mountain peaks, sleep alone in a log-cabin high in the Rockies, travel by pack-mule in savage Korea, ride two thousand five hundred miles through Persia, Kurdistan, and Armenia, visiting the Lur and Bakhtiari tribes who had fascinated Layard some thirty years previously, undertake a journey of eight thousand miles in the interior of China, of which a quarter was achieved in a small flat-bottomed boat with no shelter but a partial matting cover, and become the first European to visit the wild aborigines in Japan's northern isle.

Her first journeys to America and Canada were comparatively commonplace, although one included a tour in the Far West and a visit to wild Indians in the Hudson Bay Territory. It is noticeable that when less ambitious wanderings took her to civilized Mediterranean countries she 'returned from the trip less benefitted than her doctors had hoped'. In 1872, when she was in her forties, although she greatly bewailed the separation from her beloved sister, she decided to search for health in the Antipodes—and remained away for nearly two years. Part of her journey was in a small, crowded steamer whose decks were loaded with sheep and horses. Once in an unseaworthy boat 'danger threatened'; another time a lunatic occupied the berth next to hers; always the food was dreadful; and she found that 'heat, dust, and drunkenness' prevailed in the raw Australian and New Zealand towns. It is no surprise, therefore, to learn that when some six months later she arrived at the Sandwich Islands she was in *much* better health. . . .

She had found the panacea which was to solve her problems for the rest of her adventurous life: to be in the centre of the stage, spot-lit by distance and danger, to describe at length to an admiring circle at home the appalling situations and discomforts which she surmounted with such remarkable poise; to remove herself from all domestic ties, yet cling to them with all the strength of her stubborn nature; to remain 'a lady' but live the life of an adventurer—such contrasts almost completely obliterated from Isabella's mind the 'spinal complaint' from which she suffered in the captivity of home-life. The cosy comfort of Victorian England must have been stifling to a woman who could with equanimity share a log-cabin with two male students, camp out in the mountains with a known murderer, and sleep soundly in a hut with 'hairy Ainos'.

Her early travels in the Far West had been published by Murray under the title of *A Lady's Life in the Rocky Mountains*, and she already had a reputation as writer, lecturer, and authority on distant lands when, after a brief marriage to Dr Bishop, Isabella, now a widow in her fifties, began her great adventures.

She was a traveller pure and simple, not an explorer, a naturalist, a student of history, a missionary, or a romantic writer in search of copy. She had no vocation save a search for well-being, and her travels were undertaken for that 'novel and sustained interest which conduce so essentially to the restoration of a solitary health-seeker'. The only romance, in the accepted sense of the word, in her life is the story of Mountain Jim, the trapper she met in the Rockies and by whom she was undoubtedly attracted, but about whom she always maintained a mysterious silence. Isabella describes his face as 'smooth-shaven *except* for a beard and dense mustaches' (author's italics), of great physical beauty but disfigured on one side by a sightless eye, a gentleman born but dressed in rags, given to 'dark deeds of violence' and strong drink, but with a soft voice and chivalrous manners. Such an enigmatic figure made a great impression on one who always preferred the paradoxical to the commonplace, and when they parted it was clearly with reluctance on the part of Isabella. Obviously, however, the gentleman preferred whisky and liberty to love of the lady. Some months later, after Jim's death in a drunken brawl, his apparition appeared to Isabella in a Swiss hotel where she was staying. Always well-mannered, he merely bowed, took off his hat and was gone.

But Isabella's real love was travel, and provided she could see and do the unusual no privations were too severe to be endured by a spine which, at home, confined her to a sofa. Moreover her unlimited appetite for hearty, hirsute males, which her staid upbringing and background denied her in London or Edinburgh, could be satisfied not only without criticism, but with actual credit, in the savage countries where she loved to roam.

In the 'seventies she decided to visit Japan, then a little-known country, and to her patient enquiries about the lives and habits of the people she now added a passion for missionary work (though it is noticeable that she did none, and often sharply criticized those missions where she stayed). Only ten years earlier the Minister of the first English Legation to the Son of Heaven had been stoned in the streets of the capital; yet Isabella planned and accomplished alone a journey of hundreds of miles in the interior.

Her entry into villages was so momentous an occasion that

once no less than a thousand people gathered to gaze on the strange white woman, and crowds always surrounded her to watch her every movement. In the Japanese inns the paper screens which did duty for walls were often torn and a dark eye placed to each hole, and although she describes this as 'an oppressive lack of privacy', she stoically put up with the myriad fleas which inhabited the floor-matting, and the rats, bugs, and lice which were her daily and nightly companions, nor was she unduly squeamish about the plumbing, which in many inns consisted of a tank sunk in front of the door, sometimes emptied on the fields at night with consequent 'noxious smells'.

From Japan she sailed to the 'hermit-country' of Korea, which she at first disliked, though later she became enamoured of its wild beauty. She crossed China, India, and reached Tibet—there is no end to the remote tracks, mountain passes, deserts, and strange cities visited by this small, squat, indomitable figure, enduring without complaint the most severe privations in the wildest parts of the world, but unable to stay more than a few days in London because she found it so exhausting.

Always loath to make a home, always most lost when she was found, complaining more about the drudgery of writing her books for dear, kind Mr Murray than she ever did about hunger, dirt, or danger, Isabella Bird died in a friend's house half a century after the doctors had despaired of her health.

How different was the climate of Daisy Bates's existence! Lived under conditions of hardship which make Isabella Bird's travels appear almost *voyages de luxe*, severed from every vestige of civilization, past or present, with no letters home, no admiring circle of friends, no books to bring fame, hers was a life of self-abnegation, not a selfish search for health or sensation.

Once again it was illness which caused the traveller to go abroad. Daisy Bates was an Irish girl of good family and good looks, and her doctors prescribed Australia as the antidote for lung trouble. Here she became fascinated by the wild scenery and its wilder inhabitants, but this interest did not become an impelling force until ten years later. In the meantime she married, had a son, lost her husband, and returned to England to work with the famous editor W. T. Stead, with whom she met many late-Victorian progressive thinkers.

In 1889 stories of the ruthless treatment meted out to the aborigines in Australia shocked the nation, and Mrs Bates procured a commission from *The Times* to report on these allegations. She refuted them: she maintained that the natives were not being treated brutally but unwisely. They were being given food and clothing, both of which were unsuited to their way of life; they were being taught to copy the white man, and were punished if they did not conform to his rules, none of which they could understand. Daisy Bates realized that this was not deliberate cruelty but that it was wrong.

Now almost forty, her true life's mission began: she became absorbed in the problem of the blackfellow. She understood that it was not possible to pass from the Stone Age to the Machine Age in one generation. She realized these poor people were a doomed race and that the most that could be done was to ease their passing. For this she was prepared to give up her life, because she believed the white man owed a debt to these sad savages whose hunting grounds he had taken, and whose complicated inter-tribal laws his coming had destroyed. As another and later interpreter of the Australian scene, the poet Judith Wright, aptly said, the white man's ideals of Money, Security, and Prosperity are words of power, not words of life, and the aborigines were suffering for their non-acceptance of concepts they could not comprehend.

For a time Daisy Bates worked with the courageous Spanish Fathers who laboured in the far north-west; and she recounted with humour how a group of natives, male and female, were confirmed, all absolutely naked except for the wreath of artificial white roses and short veil worn by each in turn, which the Fathers kept for such ceremonies. She trekked a thousand miles with a head of cattle, taking her young son—the only other white person—with her, and for luggage her one portmanteau containing her English riding habit and her inevitable shirt-waist and skirt. She was attached for a time as assistant ethnologist to an expedition sent from England to study native prison conditions, and rapidly became a recognized authority on the aborigines.

When she was over fifty she decided to break altogether with Western civilization and to devote herself entirely to the natives. She set up her tent on the fringe of the great Nullabor plain, and, as the years passed, sitting round the camp-fire listening to the blackfellows' stories, she mastered over a hundred of their dialects, transcribed their legends of the 'dream-time' which constituted their only history, and accumulated a vast store of knowledge.

She never let the natives serve her; it was she who served and waited on them, went 'walk-about' and hunted for food with them, fed, encouraged, and nursed them without distinction of persons, bad or good. She never attempted to teach them the white man's ways or her own Christian beliefs, but only gave them her never-failing love and fearlessness, believing them the children of God, although they did not know Him.

She did not shrink from the most horrible blood ceremonies, understanding the importance to the aborigine of the magic power of blood. Eventually she herself was initiated and was given her due place by which she came to be known all over the vast continent. Wherever she was she could take her rightful rank, the only woman ever to be given this distinction. Even her unselfconscious narrative admits that it was a somewhat unusual sight when she stood, in her sober Edwardian coat and skirt, and sailor hat with fly-veil, in the midst of fifty savages, all entirely naked except for stripes of red ochre and white pipe-clay, crests of feathers on their heads and bottoms, and with spears in their hands.

She was not afraid of the empty spaces, the solitude, the scorching heat and terrible storms, nor of the wild animals and even wilder humans who were her only companions. She had to face the horrors of cannibalism, for the natives' favourite food was human flesh, and killing vendettas were common; but she did prohibit anyone visiting her camp to indulge in this practice, though whenever possible she helped to keep temptation away by gifts of bullock steaks. Most loathsome was their partiality for baby-meat, and she tells the gruesome story of a

DAISY BATES

as she appeared in Canberra to receive the Order of the British Empire in 1934 native woman, about to give birth, who took her young daughter and hid in the bush, and when the baby was born killed and ate it, sharing the flesh with the other child.

She survived a drought of eight years when she had to cart water two miles a day over stony tracks sometimes in a temperature of 120 degrees; and she recovered from recurring attacks of blindness which she deplored chiefly because it caused the trusting natives to query the efficacy of her magic. Very occasionally even her health and indomitable spirit gave way. Then, perhaps taking with her a couple of natives in urgent need of medical care, she would retreat to what passed for civilization at the nearest settlement, recuperate, and again return to her camp.

By some inexplicable bush-telegraph natives from all over the continent came to know of her. One woman walked a thousand miles to see the great *Kabbarli* (grandmother), who cared for the blackfellows and seemed to them an incarnation of a mysterious 'dream-time' ancestor.

Even the white authorities came to hear of her, and in 1934 she was given the Order of the British Empire. Out of the bush, after thirty-five years of solitude, came a figure from Edwardian England: shirt-waist with stiff collar and tie, long skirt and sailor hat. Although she felt herself an anachronism in the mature cities which she had last seen as raw, sprawling towns, she enjoyed the luxuries of civilized life and the pleasant intellectual association with her own kind. But she returned to the bush.

She died in 1951, aged ninety-two, poor and alone, but believing that nothing is ever lost, and that her loving magic would live on in the hearts of the aborigines and help them to keep from doing evil, lest they might hurt their beloved *Kabbarli*.

The Girl in the Baker's

JOHN MOORE

WE CALL her the girl in the baker's, though she's a girl
  no longer,
For she was a slip of a girl when we were boys.
We would stop
By her shop
And stare at her with the hunger
Of teenage hobbledehoys,
Amazed at the sight
Of a nymph or a sprite
Among cottage loaves, cheesecakes, and patties.
She didn't seem to belong
To the dull doughy world of those fatties
Her Pa and her Ma—when the girl in the baker's was young.

Sometimes it happens to girls between sixteen and twenty:
Their spring's unaccountably frosted, their primrose fades,
The spirit's stunted that gave such promise of plenty,
'A malady most incident to maids.'
Why the primrose died in Maisie we never shall know:
If it was lost love blighted her,
Or life that frighted her,
Or simply being so long among so much dough
She took of its quality, lumpish and frumpish and grey—
'Why, Maisie, I think you grow more like your mother each
  day.'

We call her the girl in the baker's; though she is nearer
Forty than thirty now, slab-faced and sour,
Satisfied rather than sorry when things get dearer;
Totting up bills, or writing an order for flour,
On purpose to keep you waiting. She does it to spite you
For having a husband or wife, or kids to delight you,
For being better off, better looking, for having more
Than Maisie—or merely for being happy though poor.

JOHN MOORE

She cultivates little queues. Standing in one this morning,
Watching her taking her time over counting the change,
Adding a bill up three times, ostensibly yawning,
Then suddenly snapping at Mrs Green from The Grange
The single word 'Yes?'—
I was trying to guess
What had happened to change her,
To sour and estrange her,
What had gone wrong.
I tried to envisage her long, long, long
Ago:
The nymph among the dough,
The sprite that wantoned and winked at us teenage loons
With noses glued to her window, ogling
And oafishly goggling
At Maisie and macaroons.

It was rather like trying to remember
Cuckoo-call in December,
Flowers out of season.
Then suddenly, for some reason,
The shop fell still.
Maisie wrote slowly a bill.
Then looking as always vaguely, shortsightedly vexed,
She cried out: 'Next!'
The customer murmured something. Then Maisie's voice again
Came to me flat and dull and doughy and plain:
'The Fancies is all gone,' she said, oh pitifully bereft;
'The Fancies is all gone,' said Maisie. 'Only the Buns is left.'

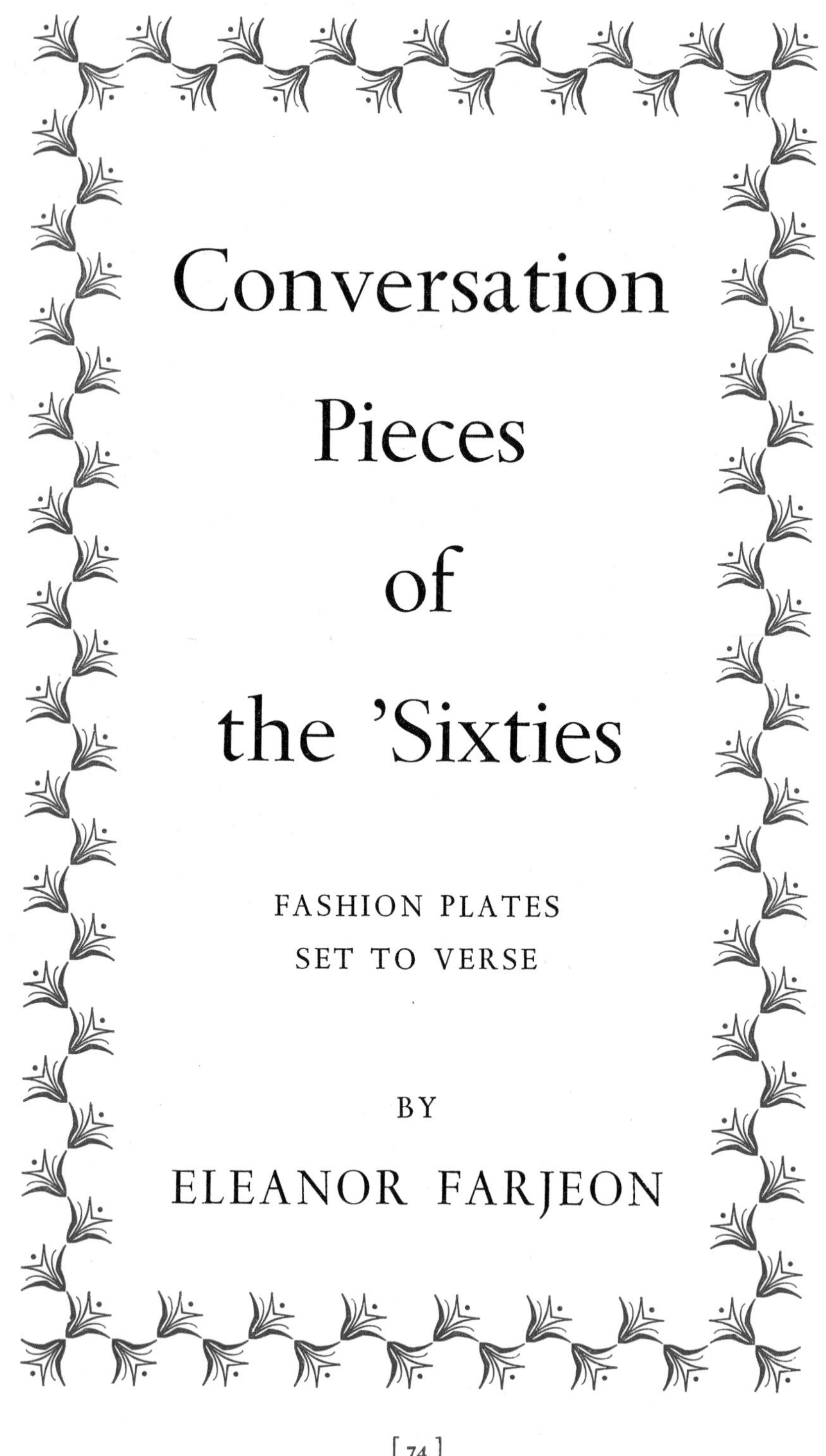

Conversation Pieces of the 'Sixties

FASHION PLATES
SET TO VERSE

BY

ELEANOR FARJEON

THE *SOI-DISANT* FRIEND

SHE IS scanning the 'house' with her glass—
The boxes, the stalls, the parterre—
The husband she dotes on (alas!)
Is he here?—is he yonder?—or where?
While behind her, her *soi-disant* friend,
Who professes to cherish her best,
Has gained her insidious end,
And implanted a doubt in her breast.

She spends not a glance on the scene,
She lends not an ear to the score,
For the monster whose optics are green
Possesses her soul to the core;
While below, on the glittering stage,
The Diva with gold in her throat
(The last metropolitan rage)
Expires on an exquisite note.

It is while the bright lights are turned down,
(Poor soul!) that she snatches her chance
To search 'mid the pleasures of town
The shards of her shattered romance;
When the blaze of the great chandeliers
Illumines her features again,
She must wreathe them in smiles, beyond tears,
And feign an enjoyment, past pain.

Suppose she should spy him—what then?
With a woman (dear God!) at his side,
Who beams on her chosen of men
As she used to beam, when a bride.
Must she suffer in silence her wrong,
And applaud, with a heart full of woe,
The roulades of the Diva of Song?—
Oh no! oh, a thousand times, no!

She will rise and denounce him: 'Lights up!
  A deceiver's among you tonight
Who has sipped the connubial cup
  And now tastes a different delight.
Behold him! A husband is he
  Whose wife is one only in name——'
But there she will falter (ah me!)
  While the shuddering house murmurs 'Shame!'

The conductor will stand in his place
  With *baton* in air, like a stone;
The bandsmen will show on each face
  A scorn that surpasses her own;
And the great Adelina will rise,
  Advance to the footlights, and call
Her 'Sister!' with tears in her eyes—
  And the curtain—the curtain will fall.

Ah, the drama enacted in 'front'
  Outrivals the stage and its play,
Where the tragedy shoulders the brunt
  While the bosoms beneath it are gay!
Is he yonder? (Oh, how will it end?)
  Or yonder? Her heart cannot rest,
For behind her her *soi-disant* friend
  Has implanted a thorn in her breast.

Fashion Plate by Heloise Leloir

THE NEW SONG

SING this one, Belinda, as sweet as it's old;
'Twill bring back fond echoes to me and to you.
No, Geraldine, no! for the melody's cold,
And here is a song as delightful as new.

Reject it, Belinda! reject with alarm
The tune that attracts you from what you held dear.
No, Geraldine, no! it has novelty's charm,
And this is the song that entrances my ear.

Be careful, Belinda! the new will not last;
The song of a season will wilt like the rose.
So, Geraldine, so did the songs of the past,
And this is as sweet as I used to find those.

In autumn, Belinda, when blue skies are grey,
You will pine to remember the ditties of spring.
That will do. They were all very well in their way,
But this is the song I am going to sing.

Fashion Plate by Heloise Leloir

SILENT COMMUNION

How spotless their dresses
  To fit the occasion!
Each toilet expresses
  Their church-going roles;
How pious, how holy
  The spirit's invasion,
When maidens go solely
  Intent on their souls.

Broderie Anglaise,
Frills at neck and wrist.
She will draw the gaze—
What a chance I've missed!
Lord! I feel so triste*!*
She will get the praise.
Frills at neck and wrist,
Broderie Anglaise.

Buttons! How demure.
Rosebuds down the skirt.
That's how she'll ensure
Victory, the flirt!
Lord! I feel so hurt!
Looks so prim and pure—
Rosebuds down the skirt;
Buttons! How demure.

White gloves and white veilings,
  And white velvet missals,
Can cover all failings
  Like snow without smirch;
But the wreaths on their tresses
  As well might be thistles.
How spotless their *dresses*
  Will go into church.

Fashion Plate by A. Poitier

Ne peut être reproduit

HE HAS SPOKEN

HE HAS spoken, dearest Mother!
He has breathed the manly word!
It is I he loves, none other,
If my ears have rightly heard;
Yet I felt such palpitation
As he poured into the night
His devoted declaration—
Could my ears have heard aright?
Ah! the sudden exaltation
When one's ears have heard aright!

There was moonlight on the water,
There was music in the grove,
As he made your only daughter
The recipient of his love.
What I said, I daren't remember!
What I felt, I scarcely know!
But my teardrop calmed the ember
Of his passion's fervent glow.
I remember too the ember
Of a passion's fervent glow!

Yes! this moment is the blossom
Of my maiden hopes and dreams;
Streaming sunlight floods my bosom
After starlight's fitful gleams.
It is I he loves, none other,
If my ears have heard aright—
Never man has spoken, Mother,
As John Harding spoke tonight!
I am thinking of another
Man and maid, another night.

Fashion Plate by Heloise Leloir

Fashion Plate by Louis Berlier

SISTER MINE

HE IS waiting over there,
  Sister mine,
With a very pensive air,
  Sister mine.
He settles and unsettles
  His cravat,
He is counting daisy-petals—
  Think of that!
When I passed, he turned his head,
Growing very very red,
And he said—but what he said,
  I divine,
Was for *your* ear, not for mine,
  Sister mine!

You had better rise and go,
  Sister mine;
He's expecting you, I know,
  Sister mine.
He's begun to fan his fever
  With his hat,
Which won't improve the beaver—
  Think of that!
When I passed, he pressed my hand,
Looking thoroughly unmanned,
But his pressure—understand?—
  Well, in fine,
Was for *your* hand, not for mine,
  Sister mine!

There! I've done the best I could,
  Sister mine,
More than other sisters would,
  Sister mine;
I've put up with the outpouring
  Of his chat,
And his sighs and looks adoring—
  Think of that!
When I passed, he plucked this flower
From the agitated shower
That adorns love's trysting-bower—
  As a sign
For a heart that wasn't *mine*,
  Sister mine!

LADIES IN LOVE

Words and Pictures collected by

 CHARLES GIBBS-SMITH 

WRITING as an old-fashioned bachelor, I must confess that the spectacle of ladies in love may evoke either dismay or delight; but, whichever it is, there is always a strong accompanying tone of astonishment, as if some sort of magic—black or white—is being performed in front of me.

In contemplating the succession of hits and misses suffered by my friends over the years, I have come to the distressing conclusion that my own sex is far more likely to confuse good and proper lust with true love. Men seldom seem mature enough to experience them together in a 'divine fusion'. Generally they believe that falling in love is synonymous with falling into bed; and they are, I am afraid, so hell bent on the latter that they feel they have to justify it by pretending—not least to themselves—that they are blissfully undergoing the former.

This failing does not seem so common among women, who seldom get confused about love and lust. But when they do fall in love they dive in at the deep end with a vengeance, and it is their magnificent lack of discrimination which leaves me so astonished. If some male happens to sport one of those supra-auditory transmitters built into his voice or his face—as some animals have—it would appear that any one of a whole range of females, attuned to the particular wavelength he broadcasts on, will start vibrating deep down within her viscera. From that moment she is a 'goner'; one can see her mounting first to a state of incandescence, then to the most abandoned devotion.

Perhaps the most dismaying aspect of this performance, to us outsiders, is that we so often have to witness the sweetest, most lovely, and most talented of women falling for the most bloody awful men—men who by any standard can only be described as rotters, cads, heels, or skunks—still the best old words. The reader is offered no prizes for cracks about jealousy. It just happens to be one of the disastrous facts of life that many of the most wonderful women in the world are captivated by cads.

An added twist to this cad-caused capitulation, which some of us meet rather early in life, is that the woman quite often dislikes and despises her cad from start to finish, yet loves him passionately. It was once classically summed up by a cad's wife, who had surfaced for a breather: 'I know he's a bastard, but I love him.' She did, too; passionately, tenderly, and devotedly, all her life. The strange thing about that couple was that one soon came to feel an indifference for the cad, but an astonished and ever-growing admiration for his lady.

In passing, one would, by contrast, pray those women who are out of love not to be ruthless and cruel to those unfortunate men—I mean the 'decent' unmolesting ones—who fall in love with them unsuccessfully. It is strange that some of the loveliest and finest women don't seem to consider it worth while acquiring the slightest skill or even simulacrum of kindness on such occasions; I have seen them strike and maim, with the ink still wet on their cheque to the Animal Protection Society.

One of the oddest of spectacles, however, is the selfishly silly woman in love, a woman who is so short-term-minded that she employs her perfectly genuine love—perhaps '*de*ploys' is the better word—to persuade her husband or lover to change his habitat, his habits, or even his job, to please her. Such a ninny's love is, of course, its own worst enemy, and heaven help this female when her male's incandescence comes inevitably to leave its owner's breast and rise to illuminate his brain.

But to compensate us spectators for such frequent dismay is the occasional spectacle of those ladies in love who get as good as they give. Such lucky ones discover—surely sometimes unbelievingly—that the difference between love and lust in the male is simply the corny one of giving or getting. It is perhaps not strange that one can always tell in a flash when a woman—be she a plain Jane or dishy dodo—has discovered this. She undergoes a transfiguration which baffles description, a transfiguration which informs the curve of her finger as surely and revealingly as it does the myriad subtleties of her face. Such a spectacle makes it just worth while staying alive.

At night—wear white.

Official traffic poster

Il fait bien avoir deux cordes à son arc. FRENCH PROVERB

'Showing a Preference', by J. C. Horsley, R.A. *Collection of Sir David Scott*

I am arrayed, I am prepared . . . I feel a thousand capacities spring up in me. I am arch, gay, languid, melancholy, by turns. VIRGINIA WOOLF

In general, one curve osculates another when it has the highest possible order of contact with the second curve.

LONEY'S *Co-ordinate Geometry*

She took the kiss sedately.

TENNYSON

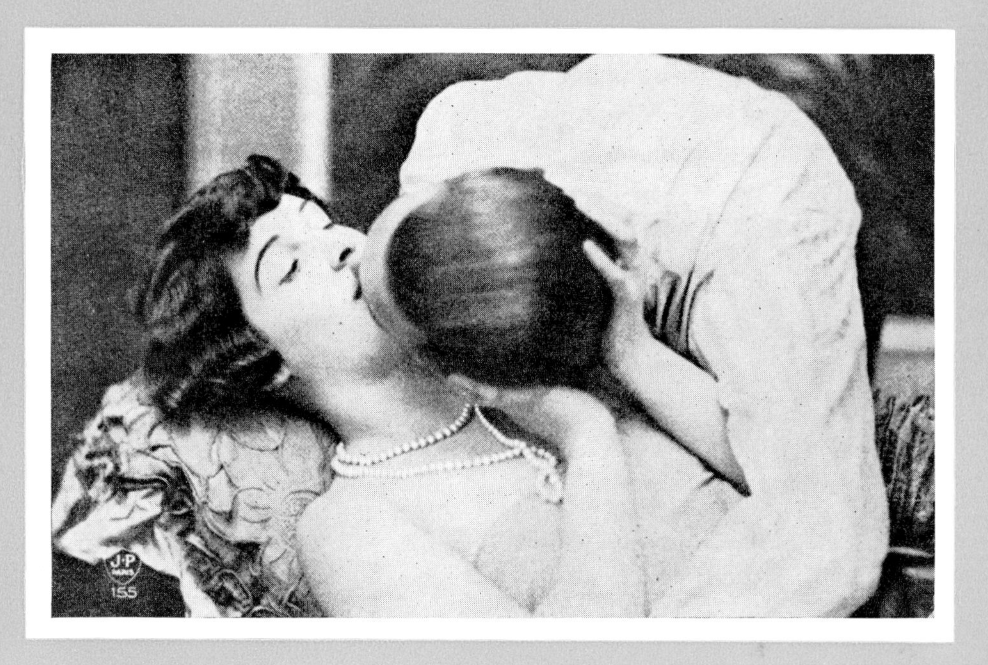

'Propinquity does it', as Mrs Thornburgh is always reminding us.

MRS HUMPHRY WARD

I would long for martyrdom in such moments of exaltation.
MADAME D'AGOULT

Every arrow that flies feels the attraction of earth. LONGFELLOW

That love which was her doom . . . TENNYSON

I'm lovely as a dream in stone, O Mortal!
I hate all movement breaking beauty's line,
And never do I laugh and never weep.

BAUDELAIRE

For a woman to receive a man in her bedroom at an hotel is to break an important convention . . . It places both in a false position.

LADY TROUBRIDGE

Surely thy body is thy mind,
For in thy face is nought to find.

ROBERT BRIDGES

I wanted warmth and colour,
which I found in Lancelot.

TENNYSON

She loves you—yeah, yeah, yeah! THE BEATLES

I love you: I'll cut your throat for your own sake. BEAUMONT & FLETCHER

Do as other widows—buy
yourself weeds, and be cheerful.

JOHN GAY

These widows, Sir, are the most perverse creatures in the world.

ADDISON

A canter is the cure for every evil. DISRAELI

The stables are the real centre of the household.

BERNARD SHAW

O my princess! true she errs,
But in her own grand way.

TENNYSON

Let us stay
Rather on earth, Beloved.

ELIZABETH BARRETT BROWNING

It is extremely rude and unkind to 'cut' an acquaintance publicly by staring coldly in response to a courteous bow and smile.

LADY TROUBRIDGE

This type of feminine emancipation can be effective also on the erotic level.

SIMONE DE BEAUVOIR

He only says, 'Good fences make good neighbours.' ROBERT FROST

'The Tryst', by F. Stone. *By courtesy of Messrs Agnew*

Shall We Dance?

JOHN PITT

IN 1919 THE Original Dixieland Jazz Band opened at the London Hippodrome. For one night only did they play, and then they were driven from the stage by an apoplectic George Robey, who offered the management a choice: Him or them? But by then the sound had been heard; the new jazz had arrived, and a war-weary, dance-crazy Britain was about to fox-trot and charleston its way into its own little aspirin age.

An understanding of the trend which modern dancing has taken since then necessarily involves a study of the development of jazz; for jazz rhythms are interwoven with nearly all the dance steps of the last fifty years. Most of us now know how jazz originated in New Orleans and worked its way up the Mississippi by river boat to Chicago, thence to New York, and finally across the Atlantic to Europe. When it reached Britain its effect was to accelerate a transition in dancing style which had begun even before the First World War.

When the Original Dixieland Jazz Band came to Britain dance styles were undergoing a radical change. Only ten years earlier the waltz had predominated in all the ballrooms. But already younger interests had begun to break away from the courtly steps which expressed the emotions and social attitudes of the previous century. Dancers had begun to 'feel' the dance, to listen to the melody rather than to perform a set of steps in tempo to the music. Perhaps it was the tango which started it. Its sinuous grace and warm exotic cadences cut at the roots of an art which stemmed from outmoded ballet forms. And, being a 'walking' dance, it offered entirely fresh scope for lateral movement. But it needed space; and on the crowded floors of smart, wartime dance clubs space was at a premium. Moreover, the atmosphere and pace were wrong for the hurried furloughs of officers who might never again clasp a girl in their arms. Instead there grew in popularity another dance from the U.S.A., the fox-trot (named after the American vaudeville comedian

Harry Fox); and with it the one-step, the two-step, and the slightly suggestive hesitation waltz. By the Armistice the old pre-war dance forms had been fragmented almost beyond recognition by such varieties of fox-trot as the Bunny Hug, the Chinese Toddle, the Turkey Trot, and the Suzie Q.

Such then was the generation to whom the Original Dixieland Jazz Band came to play in 1919. The unfortunate episode at the Hippodrome proved only a minor set-back. From there they transferred to the Palladium; then to Martan's restaurant, where neo-hedonists ate cream cakes between fox-trots at the now fashionable tea-dances. They played the new music at the Savoy's great Victory Ball; they played it before King George at the Palace. And on one memorable night over five and a half thousand dancers packed into that other palace—the new Palais de Danse at Hammersmith. When the band sailed for the States at the end of thirteen weeks they had made seventeen hit recordings and left behind a nation of devotees to Dixieland.

Several English bands sprang up in emulation of these young men from New Orleans. By 1920 Harry Roy was playing his first professional engagement as saxophonist for his brother, in Syd Roy's Lyricals. In the Strand the impeccable Debroy Somers was enchanting the Savoy supper clientele with a cultivated ragtime version of 'Yes, We Have No Bananas'. Jack Hylton succeeded Paul Whiteman at the Grafton Galleries, promoting a new form of orchestrated jazz which Whiteman had already marketed successfully in the States. As music it wasn't jazz; but as a money-spinner it was to net a small fortune for Hylton and others like him. In the same year as the O.D.J.B. barnstormed their way through Britain a young ex-army officer who had never had a dancing lesson in his life was given his first job at a pound a week in a Kensington dance salon. His name was Victor Sylvester. It says something for this tyro that within three years he had not only won the World Ballroom Dancing Championship but was running a dance studio of his own.

We tend to think affectionately of Victor Sylvester as Mr Quick-quick-slow, the Maestro of Strict Tempo Dancing. But he is much more than that. He is the man whose neat, methodical mind codified the innumerable dancing techniques of the early dancing years into one huge ballroom syllabus. His influence has been immense, but aesthetically questionable. Whilst he has greatly widened that sector of society which finds friendship and enjoyment on the ballroom floor, he has also neutered the spirit of jazz by producing a species of dippers and swoopers and featherers to whom mere style is paramount. And he has done this by stopping the dancer from listening to the music. His strict tempo offers little but a steady four-to-the-bar rhythm, filleted of the excitement and spontaneity of early ragtime.

Of course, the dance teachers of that day—or since—didn't much influence the actual trend of dancing. They only canalized the innovations into safe and easy steps for the inexperienced and inhibited. The innovations themselves came mostly from cabaret and vaudeville. The Charleston originated in the ragtime musical *Shuffle Along*, and reached Paris, from America, in the mid-'twenties. From there it was brought to London by two exhibition dancers, Bobby Sielle and Annette Mills (of *Muffin the Mule* fame), who danced it for the first time ever in Britain at Ciro's in 1926. It was exactly right for the mood of the time. Perhaps nothing has contributed so much to the pattern of later dancing as the four or five years when this extraordinary dance was in vogue. In ballrooms every other number was a Charleston. New dance schools opened every week. New bands supplied a continuous stream of orchestrated jazz; and for Jack Payne, Jack Hylton, Carroll Gibbons, Harry Roy, Ambrose, and Joe Loss, to name but a few, the going was good.

By the 'thirties the impetus had slackened, although the dancing habit itself continued unabated in the many Mecca ballrooms which now patterned the country. The zest had gone from it. Night after night banks of chromium-plated saxophones transcribed the phrases of American big-band swing into sentimental clichés, pumping out thick, rich, close-harmony chords like some musical chocolate sundae.

Yet, even as early as 1932, the influence which was to help silence this unhappy sound was already with us. As the tango had done twenty years earlier, the rumba, when it arrived, communicated to those screen-gazers from the centre stalls the excitement and exoticism of a country they knew very little about, Latin America. Xavier Cugat and Carmen Miranda became household words. 'South of the Border Down Mexico Way' was part of every errand boy's repertoire. A Mr Gerald Bright rechristened himself Geraldo and formed a gaucho band. By the beginning of the Second World War Britain was ready for the samba and Edmundo Ros. And then, immediately after it, the Charleston returned and jazz was with us again.

Jazz—that is, true jazz as played long ago in New Orleans—had seemed to have died. But in fact it had been hibernating, buried beneath the commercial compost of Tin Pan Alley. After the Second World War it stirred itself, prodded into activity by a young society for whom the orchestrated insincerities of big-band swing held no attraction. Thus entered the traditional jazz revival, the remarkable time of jive and rock-'n'-roll, when the cellars of Leicester Square and Oxford Street were filled nightly by a frenzy of jumping, cavorting girls and boys—looking (as Humphrey Lyttelton himself once put it) like nothing so much as the mating of angry flamingoes. And, curious thing, the music was played by the participants themselves, listened to repeatedly on ancient records, faithfully phrased and harmonized to the original Creole jazz sounds.

But, although the emotions were the same, the attitude was different. The hedonists and nihilists of the first post-war era—the funsters, cynics, and *choquistes*—were gone. Instead, a generation of rebels and marchers and angry young people danced enthusiastically to song-titles considered a society joke in the 'twenties: 'Margie', 'I Wish I Could Shimmy Like My Sister Kate', 'Livery Stable Blues', 'Ostrich Walk'; danced also to movements of indescribable intricacy, set within a framework that allowed for even greater individuality than the old fox-trot.

Today this generation has almost passed into maturity, and has been succeeded by a cleaner, neater, more sophisticated genre, that twists and shouts, and hitch-hikes and bossanovas and madisons—watched with envy, perhaps, by its elders, but also with keen interest by the dancing teachers, who even at this moment are adapting those crazy impulsive steps to the hesitant feet of the 'square' and aged.

Surprisingly enough, this picture was taken only a few years after that on page 108. It underlines the fact that most of the dances popular in Britain between the wars originated in the United States. This one is the Lindy Hop (named after Lindbergh's Atlantic flight in 1927). It took nearly thirty years for its European equivalent to appear in the London cellar clubs of Oxford Street and Leicester Square.

On the left: the band which started
revolution in 4/4 time. During thei
short stay the O.D.J.B. changed th
whole course of British dance music
Other bands quickly followed suit
Ted Lewis, also from America (*middl*
left); Roy Fox (*below*) who played a
the Monsignor in Piccadilly durin
the early years of the 'twenties; an
the Savoy Havana Band shown at th
bottom of the page in a pose charac
teristic of the time.

Above: a picture which reflects the spirit of the age. The time is 1921, the place the Criterion. A few years before, many of the men would have been serving in the mud of Flanders. Now the habit of reckless gaiety acquired during hurried furloughs lives on into the post-war years. Snowball fights would hardly have featured ten years previously. But the mood and music which produced the Grizzly Bear and the Bunny Hug had eaten into that Edwardian heritage. It was an era which saw the birth of the clubs and cabaret restaurants: Chez Henri, Victor's, Rector's, and the Florida, with its glass floor, and a white telephone on every table.

On the left: Carroll 'Hello Everyone' Gibbons who in 1927 succeeded Debroy Somers as leader of the Savoy Orpheans.

Some say that Paul Whiteman (*abov*
was the father of the English fox-trot. H
was certainly the first big band to arrive
Britain. The O.D.J.B. and Alexander's Ra
time Band had prepared the way. It r
mained for Whiteman to produce the slic
showmanship and sophistication that ban
leaders have emulated ever since. Whit
man was a brilliant arranger, but the soun
he produced was as far from true jazz
Irving Berlin is from Jelly Roll Morton.

On the left: Jack Hylton, and a more recen
picture of Ted Heath and his Musi
Below: Joe Loss and his band. These thre
are typical of the band-leaders who, in th
course of twenty years, followed to succe
the Whiteman formula of orchestrate
jazz.

Tommy Kinsman (*above*) is a legend in himself. Starting in the 'twenties he has, over the years, succeeded in identifying himself with all that's pop in Tops. Deb dances and Hunt Balls are his terrain. On the other hand skiffle, forerunner of the Mersey Sound, entered (and always stayed) several social notches further down.

In the late 'thirties the jitterbug craze in America seemed to have taken dancing to the nadir of idiocy. In Britain it never really arrived. Jive, its successor, rose to popularity in Britain in the post-war years, along with the Traditional Jazz revival. The picture on the left shows 100 Oxford Street during the New Look era.

Humphrey Lyttelton (*above, left*), the old Etonian son of an Eton housemaster, broke through into the classless society enjoyed by jazz musicians to become himself an acknowledged leader. He and his band produced records that some critics found indistinguishable from the original New Orleans sound of a quarter-century earlier. Also above is Acker Bilk (shown here at the Beaulieu Jazz Festival with the veteran trumpeter Nat Gonella); both played a considerable part in the revival of Traditional Jazz in Britain

On the right is Victor Sylvester, of the B.B.C.'s famous Dancing Club (*seen above*), celebrating his twenty-five years as an E.M.I. artist. As a dancing teacher he had noted that bands played music at tempos to suit the tune. He formed a pick-up group to put correct dance tempos on to records. Since that day in 1934 he has sold over thirty million records.

MARY MARGARET REVELL AND HER ROOM-MATES. *Evening News photo*

Room-Mates

MARY MARGARET REVELL

AT PARTIES people note that I am not English, though not always from my accent can they judge I am American. They ask if I am living here in London. I tell them yes, with two American room-mates, or 'roomies' as the term is used in the States. Sometimes they leave off the questions at this point. But I love to watch the expressions on people's faces when, pursuing this line of question further, they discover that my room-mates both have magnificent fur coats, are only babies, and swim like—well, like otters. And that is what they are.

Their next remark goes something like this: 'But they don't *really* live in your house. You keep them in a pen, outdoors, don't you?'

'Oh no,' I reply, 'they live in my house.'

'Extraordinary!' they exclaim.

Admittedly, life is a little different from the ordinary, living with two otters; they dominate everything and everyone, especially me. I used to have a bedroom, a very feminine one, with a pretty bedspread and eiderdown. Now it is a playroom for otters, and they sleep under the bed. Moreover, they have their own blankets, and they stole my bedspread to take under the bed, for their own. I don't have good blankets on my bed because they have made holes in strips in them so that they can play hide-and-seek in the various levels of blankets. I don't have good sheets since they often bring me presents from the garden: worms, smooth stones, occasional weeds, and, if they can find them, a slug or two.

At night I am allowed to make my bed and get ready for sleep. But, the last thing before I go to bed, there must be a romp of hide-and-seek, up and down the hall, on to the bed, behind the doors, and into the cupboards. Then we all settle down for the night, they under the bed, and I in it.

Just so I don't forget them in the night, they have a favourite trick of lying on their backs and reaching up with their paws to pull the bed springs down to their tummies. Then they let go, with a *whizz*! Since they are lying just under my head, they generally score a bull's eye into my ear. Then they bury themselves in their blankets. They spent ages pulling all the stuffing out of the springs, just so they could amuse themselves at night with this trick.

In the mornings I generally get at least one paw slapping me in the face to wake me up. This is accompanied by a gentle, persistent, throaty 'Hunk . . . hunk, hunk . . . hunk', etc. If I pretend to be asleep Munkles will get down from the bed, climb upon a chair, go from there to the top of the dressing-table in front of the window, and pull the curtains back to let the light in. She is sure to do this on Monday mornings, because she can talk to the dustmen when they come to collect, just outside the window. Then I pull the covers over my head, which is just what Munkles was waiting to see. In three jumps she is back on the bed, squiggling (a squiggle is an otter's wiggle) under the covers and pinching (with her teeth) my behind, until I jump out of bed, loudly muttering: 'O.K.! O.K.! You win. I'll come and get your breakfast.'

In the meantime Hump-a-Dump, who loves his sleep, waits until breakfast is on the plate before he makes his way, yawning, down the hall to the kitchen. He is very spoiled, and prefers to lie on his back and be fed. But he is so grateful, and so very lovable, one doesn't mind waiting on him. Then he leads the way out to the garden, where he climbs on to his 'throne', a swing, and surveys his domain.

Munkles, as usual, has gulped down all her food. Unlike Hump-a-Dump, who relishes every mouthful, I seldom can see how she even tastes her food, as it must by-pass her mouth in the rush to her stomach. She has, and uses to the fullest extent, all the push and rush and cleverness in the family. Her ultimate trick to get me up for breakfast, all else failing, including the pinching, is to go to the kitchen, jump into the drinking pan, and return to my bed to spank my face with wet paws and dry her cold, wet fur on my face. She has made it only once, all the way on to the bed . . . the first time she was in this condition.

After playing in the garden they come into the house to go swimming in their 'pool' . . . which used to be my bathtub. Every once in a while I am still allowed to use it for my own bath purposes. But I must use great strategy, because sharing a bath with a nearly full-size otter can have complications. And they resent my not having any toys to play with.

They have all kinds of toys in the water with them: a yellow plastic lemon, which they try to push under the water, a pink plastic whale, which they have chewed holes in so he will sink, a hard plastic ball, which they can toss into the air while lying on their backs floating, and tin cans of various sizes that make noises when banged against the side of the tub. It is a special joy to see them swimming: rolls and twists and turns, dives and leaps from the bottom, and flips into the air. Wet poetry, I call it.

When my 'roomies' have finished their bath (and even I in a 'beauty soak' never spend so much time in the water) they pull the plug out, carry it through the water, and leave it on the bench next to the bath. Throughout their water games they have been jumping in and out of the bath, running up and down the hall, running outside, and generally making a mess. If I'm not careful to watch they will take a second bath in the best 'swimming pool' they have yet discovered: the loo. In fact, left alone on their own, they will put as many of their toys as they can find into it. Thank heavens they can't work the handle . . . yet.

My otters have their own towels. And they dry themselves to a beautiful, glossy burnished brown and silver. Then comes their own private romp, when I seldom intrude, as they play 'Run, Jump, Bite, and Run'. This is a special otter game, played either while drying off, or by jumping in and out of their 'toddlers' trolley' in their room. The idea is to run as fast as possible, fly through the air at the last minute, land and tackle the opponent, give a good bite, and then escape quickly.

They don't include me in this game, because they try to be as careful with me as they can. Sometimes they forget themselves, and in the excitement of their play unintentionally get a little rough. Their own skin is so tough they seldom get hurt. They have never hurt anyone, though, for it just isn't in their nature to be unkind.

Keeping my room-mates in food gets to be a problem. They have a very fast rate of digestion, preferring to eat often in the day, in small quantities, using up about four pounds of minced beef every thirty-six hours. But this isn't all they eat. Twice a week they consume a bowl of milk, and daily have at least one raw egg. Tomatoes rank very high, along with hard-boiled eggs, among favourite foods that they like to 'snitch'. This is done by opening the refrigerator door whenever my back is turned, if I have been careless and left the door un-wired. Not only do they know how to open it, but they always close it behind them. It is one of those things which they know will always elicit a response from me.

If they feel I am ignoring them there are several steps they take to draw attention to themselves. They first go up and down the hall making their hard-luck sound, which is a pitiful little squeak, well designed to bring me running with open arms, ready to play with them. If I am working, however, they find it much better to go to the door and scratch at it frantically, crying and crying. The secret is to never give up . . . I can be worn down. That failing, they go to the refrigerator; even if it is wired shut, it is worth the try. Just the sound of the door opening and banging shut will at least get me to scold them. If all these things are ineffectual the best way to draw my attention is to jump on to the telephone table and begin loudly playing with the dial. They then push it slowly . . . slowly, across the table, making as much noise with the receiver as possible. If they feel I really deserve punishment they push it quickly off the table on to the floor, and then run for their lives and hide under the bed.

They find the telephone a wonderful toy. They dial on it; the receiver is fun to knock off the hook; and there are lots of buttons to push. But the most fun of all is when it rings. Sometimes, when I am out, and the telephone rings, it seems that they knock the receiver off the hook so that they can hear a voice saying: 'Hello . . . hello . . . hello.'

The telephone engineers are now good friends of ours. We usually see them once a week, particularly on Monday mornings, when the telephone has taken a weekend of punishing play. The first time I rang the engineer to tell him an otter had broken my telephone . . . well . . . !

People coming to the house to visit us find it rather strange to be told they must be careful to close or lock every door after themselves. Cupboards, for example, are one of the greatest attractions to otters. Rummaging around, they are happiest when getting into as much mischief as possible, preferably if it is in the cupboard where the dirty linen is put and household supplies are stored. They will pull all the sheets and towels out, into the hall, playing and burrowing in them like children on an autumn day frolicking in the leaves.

The most magnificent fun, though, is the roll of toilet paper. To string it up and down the hall, pushing it with their noses, mile after mile of it, is endless fun. Until, of course, Munkles, who rather spoils things at times, comes along and wads it all up in one soaking mess in her kitchen drinking bowl.

So you see, I really do have otters for room-mates, and they really did come from America. In fact, they flew to England with me on a Pan American jet, each with its own seat, and tiny seat-belt, made to size.

And despite the inconvenience, the messes, having to keep cupboards bolted shut, the refrigerator wired shut, and the bathroom door locked, and my bed made with otter-proof bedding, and living throughout even the winter days with my back door open to the garden, and working all my schedules around an otter time-table, they are wonderful room-mates. Most of all, I am rewarded with something which is very dear and precious to me: that rare acceptance by two animals who had no domestic traces in their heritage, and who have allowed me to glimpse new insights into a very private world.

They seem to me to be entirely happy. But perhaps they have one ambition so far unfulfilled. I am a channel swimmer and I feel that they long to teach me, sometime when I go out on a long-distance swim, to catch my own fish.

LEAVES from a Sketch Book

Malta Victorious

 DRAWINGS BY LAURENCE SCARFE 

FORTUNE gives with one hand and takes with the other; and Malta, strategically placed at the very centre of the Mediterranean, has had her share of the buffetings and counter-buffetings of empires. She has been left, however, exceedingly well stocked not only with astonishing amounts of old armour and guns but with loads of valuable furniture, rich stuffs, paintings, and tapestries, and all the other decorative accoutrements of the vice-regal and aristocratic life her protectors brought with them to make existence more tolerable between sieges and wars.

Though they were both faced with the same problems, the Maltese and their protectors always found themselves in distinct social groups, but, while an essentially aristocratic officer-class set out primarily to make themselves comfortable for their own benefit, in the long run they nevertheless benefited the Maltese. They created an island civilization which because of geographical rigours and the ever-present threat from the ardours of the blazing sun might have remained a hard place to live in without outside help.

Ever since those dreadful days of the Arab corsairs, when the Maltese were considered fit only to be shipped away in batches for slavery to Islam, the European adventurers on Malta—the French, Spanish, Portuguese, Germans, Italians, and finally the English—bestowed in no small measure a fuller cosmopolitan flavour: firstly with fantastic fortifications, dock and harbour installations, then with grandiose civic buildings and palaces, new towns and villages; thus, with the general establishment of law and order, accomplishing the peaceful progress of this beautiful island.

MALTA VICTORIOUS

So overwhelming at first sight are the foreign influences that we are bound to ask: What has been the Maltese contribution to all this? What, as regards art and architecture, have the Maltese done that can be truly called their own? And it is not till we take further scrutiny that we find that they did with continental idioms no more nor less than we British did in our own northern island—they acted as welcoming hosts, and then, by training Maltese artists of all kinds, transmogrified the styles from abroad in a charming manner according to earlier traditions, to suit their own spiritual and material requirements.

While empire-builders came and went, the Maltese quietly cultivated their own artistic gardens, so that within the limits of what is, after all, a very small island—seventeen miles long by nine wide—they find themselves today as richly endowed with good architecture and decoration as any of those choice little towns of south-eastern Sicily, or even the far-away splendours of Catholic Mexico. In fact, fortifications apart (fortifications no longer of any use!), we are mainly impressed by the arts of peace, and above all by the arts of the Counter-Reformation Church.

Today that which is of artistic importance in Malta is almost entirely—certainly in quantity—the product of artists and architects of the Baroque, a local variant of the greater European movement (colonial or provincial if you like), of island builders and craftsmen, supplemented by ever-welcome visiting artists: itinerant artists from Naples or Sicily, painters like Caravaggio who found the island at least a temporary haven from persecution, and others like Matteo Preti, who stayed here most of his working lifetime. The strong religious feelings of the Maltese, who ever since the Arabs withdrew or were assimilated have opted without question for the Church of Rome, have centred round the sumptuous churches and chapels to be found at the very heart of town and village life. Around these has grown a microcosm of festivals and observances and a characteristic folk art.

The Monument of Grand Master Nicolas Cotoner, erected in 1686, in the Conventual Church of St John, Valletta. These many monuments of bronze and marbles stand with brilliance and bravura, like clearings in the ornamental jungles of chapels.

Beyond the Porte des Bombes at Valletta a few acres of wasteland are covered with the carved capitals and ornaments salvaged from the neo-classical ruins of the Opera House —a great wilderness of stony acanthus among dry weeds.

Decorated obelisks, of gold and silver tinsel balls and dried camomile flowers dyed in primary colours, topped by plumes of pampas grass, stand with bouquets of flowers around the famous statue of Our Lady of Grace at Zabbar, at the Feast of Il-Bambina.

The Maltese *dghajsa* rides the water of Galley Creek with only slightly less grace than the gondola. Galley Creek has been somewhat prosaically named Dockyard Creek since the English occupation, but nevertheless has magnificent gold and rose-coloured waterfronts—Senglea on one side, Vittoriosa on the other, competing in scenic grandeur. This is the view of Vittoriosa.

The Church of St Paul, Rabat, begun in 1575—seen through a gap of demolitions—has great significance for the islanders as marking the spot where the Apostle preached after his shipwreck. Adjoining the main church are pleasantly cool and empty catacombs, and a small cave-chapel containing his statue.

The statue of Queen Victoria gazes benevolently in the sunshine of Queen's Square, Valletta. The pigeons treat her with familiarity, roost among the comforts of her regal draperies, and vie with each other to nestle in her crown.

he Parish Church of St Nicholas, in the main street of Siggiewi, achieves the domina-
ng verticality of a liner in dry dock. It was built in 1675, with an arcaded porch added
hundred years ago—an example of the successful persistence of Maltese baroque.

Over the hill from a stretch of dramatic country with a feeling of age-old cultivation lies the wide bay of Marsaxlokk. Here is a workaday fishing village, with the quiet excitements of painted boats, nets, cork, children, and unpretentious and colourful houses.

LAURENCE SCARFE

The Maltese scene, as it strikes the visitor, is predominantly baroque, sober in basis but lavish in detail—a near-African baroque; resplendent in the bright light outdoors, and indoors unashamedly polychromatic. Yet at the same time it remains an island art, where the rugged simplicities of fisherfolk and farmers have leavened the sophisticated idioms from abroad. The landscape is man-made, stony and bold, in which the villages lie as collections of golden cubes, each with its overriding baroque domes and ornate belfries against the wide sky. The coast is broken by unspoilt bays and dotted with tranquil colour-washed fishing villages; while as the focus of urban life stand Valletta, Senglea, and Vittoriosa, built around the great harbous which has seen so very much history.

L.S.

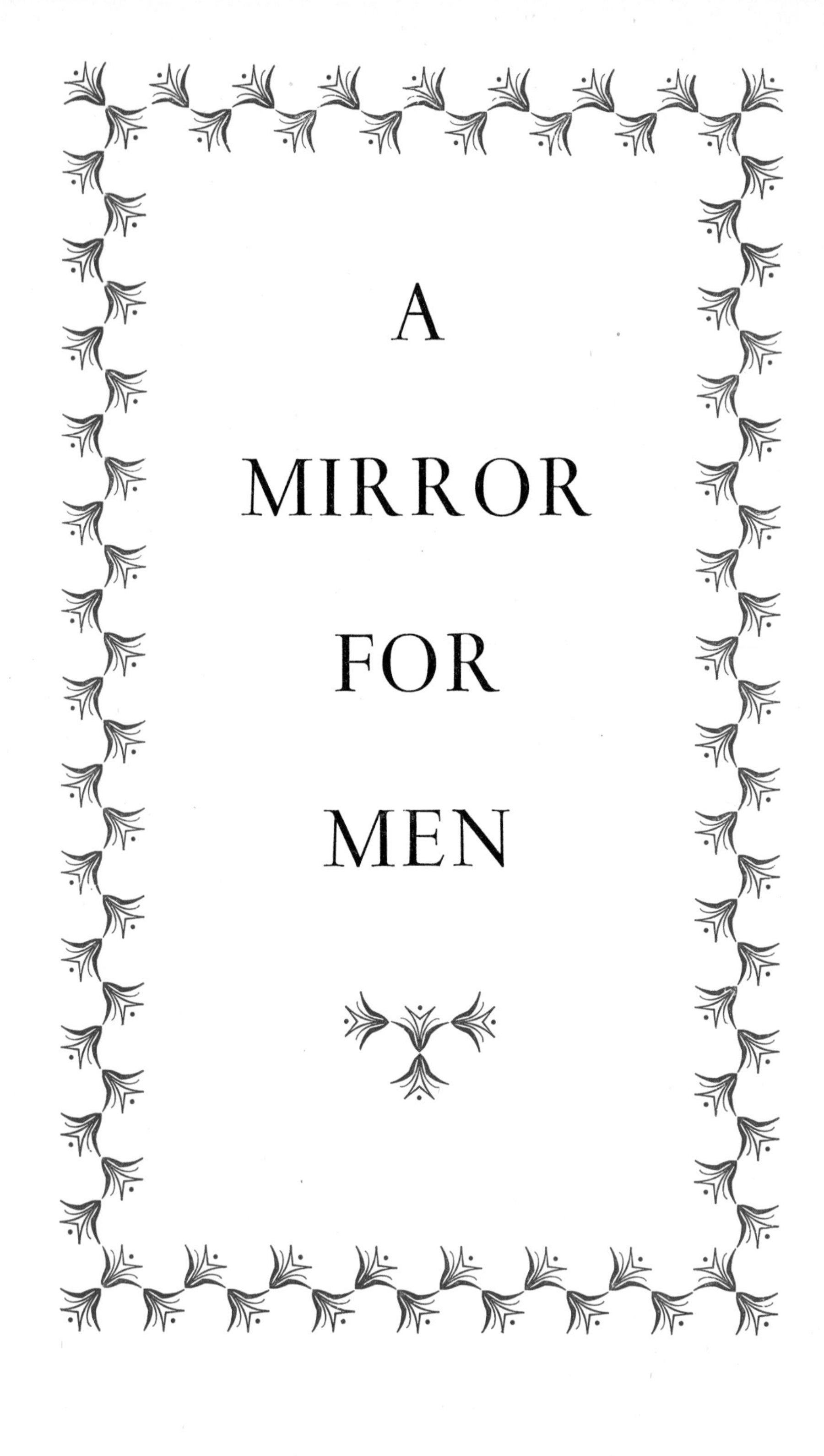

A MIRROR FOR MEN

SANDOW, THE STRONG MAN

SANDOW
The Strong Man

FRANK W. LANE

THE STRONG-MAN act is decidedly out of fashion in Britain today. Yet around the turn of the century it was a favourite on the halls, and none was more popular than Eugene Sandow's. He outstripped all his strong-armed brethren in fame. He alone has left a name for posterity.

He was born in Königsberg, Germany, in 1867, a well-formed child, but he was not particularly strong.

When he was about ten his father took him on a holiday to Rome and Florence. There they saw the finely sculptured figures of ancient athletes and wrestlers. Their lithe muscular bodies fired young Sandow's imagination. From then on the course of his life was set. He, too, would have a handsome, well-muscled body of which he could be proud.

Although he exercised himself, and frequently watched the athletes and wrestlers in the local circus-ground, he was not satisfied with his progress. Then, when he was eighteen, he went to a medical school at Brussels. His parents, who disapproved of their son's obsession with might and muscle, thought that going to Brussels showed their boy's intention, after all, to become a doctor. But, once at the school, almost the only subject he was interested in was anatomy. In that course he was the most ardent student in the place.

What Sandow wanted was to learn about the structure of the human frame; above all, its muscles. Some years afterwards he posed as a model for an anatomical class, again learning about human musculature while the lecturer discoursed on Sandow's body. In the end he knew a good deal more about human muscles than the students, and probably more than most doctors. This knowledge set him apart from the run-of-the-mill strong men.

Sandow's own strength, and the lessons he prescribed for a multitude of pupils, were based on a thorough knowledge of human anatomy. He wrote:

> I ascertained the best means of developing the body, and invented the system of giving each individual muscle a movement, and of so arranging the form of the exercises that when some muscles are brought into play others are relaxed and left without strain.

Sandow already had the determination to become a strong man; now he had the knowledge, and only practice was needed. By the time he was twenty he was strong enough to perform in public. About this time he went to Holland, trying to sell his strong-man act to theatres in Amsterdam. But nobody wanted him. Soon his resources were almost gone, he owed money at his hotel, and some of his belongings were in pawn.

Then he hit on an idea for attracting publicity, the first of a number of publicity efforts which studded his career. Dotted about Amsterdam were numbers of 'Try your Strength' machines, in which the would-be strong men inserted a coin, then pulled on a handle. This caused a needle to record the strength of the pull on a dial—50 pounds, 80 pounds, 100 pounds, and so on. Sandow found that with a hefty pull he could not only send the needle right round the dial, but also wreck the mechanism and wrench out the handle, leaving it dangling from its chain.

On several nights he went round the city, doing just this. The owners of the machines complained to the police, saying that a gang of hooligans appeared to be wrecking their livelihood. The police went on extra night duty to protect the remaining machines. But this didn't stop Sandow. The publicity all this caused was, of course, just what he wanted. And when, about ten o'clock one night, he was eventually caught—in the very act—he went quietly to the police station, followed by an excited crowd. Yes, he alone was responsible; no gang was involved; but what had he done wrong? He had paid his money and tried his strength as the machines invited him to do. Was it his fault if they were not strong enough?

The police released him. The crowd clamoured for further

demonstrations of his strength. But Sandow went quietly home; he would not now starve. Within twelve hours he signed a lucrative contract to perform his act in a theatre which had previously refused him.

More strong-man acts followed in various countries—including England—and in 1893 he went to America. His fame preceded him. A New York newspaper asked Dr D. A. Sargent, an authority on athletics at Harvard University, to make a professional examination of Sandow, who was then approaching the peak of his strength. He was 5 ft. 8½ in. tall and weighed 180 pounds.

What first impressed Sargent was the great size of Sandow's muscles compared with his bones. Then Sandow had remarkable control over his muscles. One of his acts was to make various muscles move in time to music, including muscles that the vast majority of us never move voluntarily in our lives. He used to point proudly to a muscle on the outside of his leg just below the waist. Most of us don't even know we have such a muscle; on Sandow it was nearly as big as a child's cricket bat.

Sargent also found that, despite Sandow's great strength and heavy muscles, he could move surprisingly fast, having a very short reaction-time. He claimed, with some reason, that provided his knuckles were protected, he could drive his fist through a two-inch board. Sargent said: 'Altogether Sandow is the most wonderful specimen of man I have ever seen.'

But it was when the tests began that he really surprised Sargent. Sandow knelt down and laid his right hand flat on the floor, palm upward. He then asked Sargent, who weighed 175 pounds, to place one foot on it. Firmly grasping this, Sandow rapidly lifted Sargent and put him on a table, then put him down again on to the floor. This was remarkable enough, but what astounded Sargent was that Sandow performed this feat with a straight arm; there was not the slightest bending at the elbow.

If you want to know just what that means try lifting a typewriter from the floor on to a table with one hand held at arm's length. And remember that Sandow was doing this, not with an office typewriter weighing, say, twenty-five pounds, but with a man weighing seven times as much!

But I think what surprised Sargent as much as anything was what Sandow could do with his abdominal muscles. When Sandow contracted them, and a hand was rubbed against his abdomen, it felt just like corrugated iron—except that it was somewhat warmer!

To show what he could do with these muscles Sandow lay on the floor and asked Sargent to stand on his abdomen. For a moment Sandow relaxed, then he suddenly contracted the muscles—and shot Sargent into the air.

These performances, of course, were done on the spur of the moment, without benefit of apparatus or any stage props. But with the aid of these, Sandow thrilled audiences on two continents. In one act assistants struggled on to the stage with a huge bar-bell—a long metal bar ending in two large globes. Sandow lifted this with *one* hand. He held it for a few moments with his arm stretched straight out from his shoulder, then raised it above his head. On lowering it to the floor, the two globes opened and out stepped a man from each.

This was an exhibition of brute strength, but another trick involved a good deal more. Sandow took a fifty-six-pound weight in each hand, a total equivalent to four heavy typewriters. He then performed a backward somersault. Next he did the same with his eyes blindfolded and his feet tied. Finally, he knelt down, still holding the four typewriters as it were, and again somersaulted backwards, landing on his feet. Just how he did the last trick puzzles me. I am no athlete, admittedly, but without any weights at all I can just about jerk my knees off the ground, and that is all.

With one finger Sandow could lift 600 pounds. He did it by putting his finger in a metal ring embedded in a large block of stone. He could tear *two* packs of playing cards in half. When metal bracelets were fastened round his upper arm he would contract his biceps—as big as oranges—and the bracelets would fly apart. And when he was fifty years old he could still chin the bar twenty times with either hand.

All these are examples of what may be called active strength. But Sandow was, perhaps, even more impressive in feats where he used his body as a support. He balanced a heavy platform on his chest, and three horses—one in the middle, one at each end—played seesaw on it. In another act he supported a large wooden bridge, and a horse and chariot containing two men drove across it. Flo Ziegfeld, his manager in America, said that Sandow once supported him and his company of thirty-two people on his back. If the weight of these people averaged 140 pounds this means that, with the heavy platform, Sandow was supporting on his back and legs more than two tons.

Using harness and a special platform he lifted two tons. Incidentally, Paul Anderson of America has lifted two and a half tons—the equivalent of two six-seater cars.

But I should give a wrong impression of Sandow if I referred only to his strength and public displays. For nearly thirty years, from about 1896, Sandow's name was a synonym for physical fitness. There were songs about him, and a popular saying, referring to those who practised his system, was: 'As jolly as a Sandow.' In 1897 he launched a national campaign in Britain for physical development. One result was the founding of hundreds of Sandow physical-culture clubs throughout Britain.

He had an Institute near Piccadilly where he and a staff of instructors gave lessons to many thousands of people—men, women, and children. Even doctors took his course. In 1914 he received the royal warrant as instructor in physical culture, the warrant being renewed annually until his death in 1925. As far as I know, nobody else has ever been issued with such a warrant—either before or since Sandow's day. King George V used some of Sandow's appliances.

Sandow was, of course, consulted by all sorts of people, sometimes for unusual reasons. Sir George Alexander, the actor, once had a part in a play which called for him to throw a man over the side of a ship. As Sir George was not particularly strong, the feat was beyond him. He consulted Sandow, who gave him some lessons and showed him the knack of throwing bodies about. Even so, on the first night Sandow was nervous, especially when he saw that the actor who was to be thrown was particularly solid. But Sir George threw him overboard as though he had been ducking rival actors all his life.

Another unusual visitor to Sandow's Institute was the pianist, Paderewski. Sandow devised for him a system of exercises to strengthen his wrists and fingers.

What was Sandow like as a man? T. P. O'Connor, who knew him well in his later years, said he was a pleasant personality, generous and hospitable. But he was a curious mixture of shrewdness and naivety. He made a great deal of money through his Institute, but lost tens of thousands through a disastrous business venture outside his special field.

Sandow's great strength was the cause of some interesting incidents in his private life. While visiting an acquaintance, Sandow admired a large stone sculpture which his friend had in the basement of his house. His friend laughingly said: 'You can have it if you can carry it away,' probably thinking that the half-ton of stone was safe even from the strength of a Sandow. Whereupon Sandow lifted it and carried it away.

Flo Ziegfeld, who knew him intimately, said he 'was the mildest-mannered man I ever knew'. But I have come across a few incidents where Sandow was roused to use his great strength in private life. Ziegfeld tells one such story himself. He was dining with Sandow and his wife in a New York restaurant when a fellow diner, apparently somewhat drunk, insulted Sandow's wife. Sandow went over and seized him. The man gripped the table and wouldn't let go. So Sandow lifted both man and table and threw them into the street.

Another somewhat similar story: while on holiday in the south of France he was tricked by two men who robbed him of some valuable possessions. Sandow and another man went in search of them and eventually caught them in the street. Sandow pounced on them and seized each man by the back of his neck. The men struggled, so Sandow banged their heads together until one was cowed and the other knocked unconscious. He then dragged them both to the police station and flung them in front of the officers.

It was some days before the thieves were well enough to appear in court. By that time Sandow had recovered his property and declined to prefer charges against the men. He thought he had punished them enough himself.

 SANDOW: THE STRONG MAN 

I think the most remarkable incident in Sandow's incident-crowded life happened in May 1894, when he was in San Francisco. A Colonel Bone, who was exhibiting a large menagerie there, advertised that there was to be a fight between a lion and a bear. But the police and a humane society quite rightly intervened and the fight was forbidden. Sandow volunteered to take the place of the bear. To avoid bloodshed, and to make the contest one of strength alone, it was agreed that the lion should wear a heavy leather muzzle and have its claws covered.

Even so the lion could easily kill. It weighed 530 pounds against Sandow's 180 and had recently badly mauled a man. And even with its claws covered it was quite capable of literally knocking Sandow's head off with one well-connected blow.

Sandow said he thought that before the contest proper there should be a rehearsal. So a large cage, seventy feet across, was prepared and the lion was let in. The muzzling had made it mad. Sandow entered the cage stripped to the waist. There was a handful of anxious onlookers, some of whom thought Sandow was about to be killed. It is said that the face of Flo Ziegfeld was white. For what followed let Sandow speak for himself:

> The lion, with fury in his eyes, crouched down ready to spring. Having read a good deal of the methods of the lion I was not unprepared for this form of attack. As he made his last strain for a tremendous leap I stepped sharply to the side and he missed his mark. Turning quickly before he had time fully to recover, I caught him round the throat with my left arm, and round the middle with my right. I lifted him as high as my shoulder, gave him a good hug to assure him that it was necessary to respect me, and tossed him on to the floor.
>
> Thus outdone at his first attempt, the lion roared with rage. Rushing fiercely towards me he raised his huge paw to strike a heavy blow at my head. For the moment, feeling the swish of the lion's paw as it passed my face, I really thought that Colonel Bone's remark that he would knock my head off would prove true. Luckily I ducked my head just in time, and got a good grip round the lion's body, with my chest touching his and his feet over my shoulders. Now came the tussle; the more I hugged him the more he scratched and tore, and, though his feet were mittened, he tore through my tights and parts of my skin. But I had got him as in a vice, and his efforts to get away were fruitless. Choosing an opportune moment, I flung him off me, Colonel Bone and my manager shouting to me to come out of the cage, as I had done enough, and the lion's rage was unbounded.

I was determined, however, before I left to try just one other feat. Moving away from the lion, I stood with my back towards him, thus inviting him to jump on me. I had not to wait many moments. He sprang right on my back. Throwing up my arms I gripped his head, then caught him firmly by the neck, and in one motion, shot him clean over my own head to the ground. Colonel Bone rushed into the cage, snapping two revolvers to keep the lion off, and I came out, my legs torn, my neck bleeding, and with scratches all over my body; but I felt that I had mastered that lion, and that I should have little difficulty in mastering him again at the performance that was to be given next day in public.

On the night of the fight the huge tent was packed—some reports say that twenty thousand people were there. A preliminary flurry of excitement occurred when the lion broke free from its handlers and caused a stampede among those near at hand. But it was captured and eventually entered the cage, Sandow coming in soon after.

What followed was crashing anticlimax. Sandow had won the fight at rehearsal; the lion knew he was its master and wanted no more fight. It lay on the ground. The only sign of fight it showed was when Sandow twitched its tail. Then it bounded towards him, but Sandow dodged, picked it up and tossed it contemptuously to the ground. Then he picked it up and put it on his shoulders, where it remained quiet as a lamb while he carried it round the arena.

There is controversy about a number of incidents in Sandow's life. I have relied mainly on Sandow's own writings and a biography of him which he approved.

The World of Charles Hamilton

ROBERT KELLY

ALTHOUGH the creator of Billy Bunter was the most productive writer of school stories—and stories of schoolboy adventure—of this century, recognition of his talents came almost by accident. Ironically, it also came when he had passed his peak as a writer.

Charles Hamilton worked for fifty-five years under various pen-names. His output totalled 40,000 to 60,000 words a week for several decades. Those now legendary boys' weeklies, *The Magnet* and *The Gem*, with their stories of Greyfriars and St Jim's, owed their success to him, for in addition to creating two of the most famous schools in fiction, he also wrote the majority of their stories over a thirty-three-year period.

When George Orwell singled out the two papers for lengthy

criticism in his famous essay 'Boys' Weeklies', published in *Horizon* in 1940, he could not have known how personal his attack on Hamilton was. Like other critics he assumed that a team of writers was responsible for the stories. Hamilton could not resist replying, and in doing so revealed for the first time that he was 'Frank Richards' of *The Magnet* and 'Martin Clifford' of *The Gem*. When the dust of the dispute had settled both papers had ceased publication owing to the newprint shortage.

The suspension of publication of the two weeklies was a bitter blow to Hamilton, then in his late sixties. Throughout the 1920s and 1930s he had probably earned between £3,000 and £4,000 a year, and it might reasonably have been thought that he would have welcomed his enforced retirement. But Hamilton was both a born writer and one of life's perpetual gamblers. He neither wanted to retire nor had he the means to do so.

After the war there was no attempt to revive the two magazines, which had probably lost some of their popularity even before 1939. Hamilton, now in his seventies, bravely launched out as a writer of hard-cover books and paperbacks. He revived Tom Merry and Co. from *The Gem* and even created new characters and new schools. But it was the thirty or more Billy Bunter books that he produced between 1947 and his death in 1961 that brought him real fame.

They were issued under his favourite pseudonym 'Frank Richards' and were to some extent a continuation of the Greyfriars saga, complete with the familiar cast—Bunter, Harry Wharton, Bob Cherry, Vernon Smith, Mr Quelch, Coker, etc.—from *The Magnet*. More surprisingly, Hamilton also wrote the scripts of the Billy Bunter television plays. The TV series helped to boost the sale of the yellow-jacketed Bunter books, which today are as familiar a sight on newsagents' or children's library shelves as Biggles or William.

The post-war Billy Bunter books are competently written, consistently entertaining, and owe little to nostalgic memories of *The Magnet*. And perhaps this is why they are not too popular with the many adult collectors of *The Magnet*. At any rate, collectors largely agree that not only did the best Greyfriars stories appear between the blue and yellow covers of *The Magnet* in the late 1920s and early 1930s, but that by comparison even the later *Magnet* stories show a lower standard of performance.

There are other reasons why the earlier Greyfriars stories may be considered superior to the hard-cover Bunter books. First it can be argued that the post-war stories are often rehashes of themes originally used in *The Magnet*. Then there is the question of length. The finest *Magnet* serials often ran to 350,000 words, or even longer, compared with the compact 65,000-word Bunter books. While the length of a story is obviously no criterion of quality, there is little doubt that a broad canvas suited Hamilton best. He needed room for his subtle characterization, his (deceptively) large casts, his endearing mixture of comedy and drama, and his complicated plots and sub-plots. The success of his methods can best be seen in *The Magnet*, where he created a world as believable—according to the aims of the author—as the London of Dickens and Trollope's Barsetshire.

Perhaps the most serious criticism one can make of the post-war Bunter books is that they are limited to the light-hearted type of story suitable as a showcase for Greyfriars' most celebrated pupil. It is not generally realized today that *The Magnet* featured within its pages every type of story possible in a school or holiday setting without resorting to the fantasy of visits to lost valleys filled with prehistoric monsters, invisible schoolboys, magic potions, or feats of superhuman strength. If there was a touch of fantasy about the Greyfriars scene it was merely of the type that made the settings and characters seem a little larger than life.

At least two other characters, the flawed hero-figure Harry Wharton and Vernon Smith (always on the verge of expulsion, as George Orwell remarked), rivalled Bunter in popularity, and were featured in long dramatic series in which there was far less Bunter than usual. While the summer and Christmas holiday series were good vehicles for Bunter, it is interesting to note that one such story, the 1927 South Seas series, bears far more resemblance to Robert Louis Stevenson's *Treasure Island* than to any post-war Bunter adventure. And *The Magnet* tale can stand comparison even with *Treasure Island* remarkably well.

The Magnet was first published in 1908, as a companion to the year-old and very successful *Gem*. The main feature of both papers was the school story which Hamilton wrote under his two famous pen-names. From the first, and contrary to instructions, the author made the Greyfriars stories different from the St Jim's tales in *The Gem*. There was a greater emphasis on personal conflict than on house or school rivalry, and many of the best *Magnet* stories were set away from the school locale. From the first *The Magnet* had a stronger cast of characters.

However, up to 1914 Hamilton continued to produce the bulk of his best work for the older-established *Gem*. The First World War brought changes of editorial policy, and Hamilton began to write for other Amalgamated Press weeklies—he created Rookwood School for *The Boys' Friend*—while stories by substitute authors glutted *The Magnet* and *The Gem*.

In the early 1920s Charles Hamilton was once again working regularly for the two weeklies, but substitute stories continued to appear. In a sense Hamilton had become too successful for his own good. He was now the star boys' paper author of the Amalgamated Press, which was feeling the pinch of competition from the Dundee firm of D. C. Thomson with their *Wizard*, *Adventure*, and *Rover*—followed a few years later by *Hotspur* and *Skipper*. Hamilton's work was in demand to keep up the flagging circulations of the older Amalgamated Press weeklies, or to get new papers like *Modern Boy* and *Ranger* off to a good start.

Against this background it was obvious that he would never again be able to give the same concentrated attention to both *The Magnet* and *The Gem* as before. Some time during 1926 the decision was finally made (perhaps at Hamilton's own insistence) that *The Magnet* at least should have first call on his services.

This change of policy was unfortunate for *The Gem*, which was already lagging behind *The Magnet* in the circulation race. More and more stories by substitute authors appeared, until they dominated the scene. There is some evidence that circulation declined still further during this period, and in 1931 the bold decision was made to reprint the early *Gem* stories from 1907 onwards. The reprints were so successful that they lasted eight years. The vast majority of these stories were, of course, by Hamilton. Only in the last nine months of its career did *The*

Gem publish original stories once more. And this time there were no substitute authors.

The switch to *The Magnet* in 1926 resulted in an immediate and sustained improvement in the standard of the Greyfriars stories. Between 1927 and 1935 *The Magnet* presented a first-class sequence of tales which represent Hamilton's best work in a writing career of seventy years, and he continued to write regularly for the paper until it ceased publication in 1940. It was mainly

during this period that he developed Billy Bunter from an eccentric and enjoyable character into one of the immortals of literature, a personality who, like Sherlock Holmes, Mr Micawber, or Mr Toad, seems to have a life of his own, independent of his creator.

It is indeed impossible to speak of *The Magnet* without giving Bunter a good deal of attention. His fame is international. The name immediately conjures up a picture of a fat and fatuous boy wearing tight check trousers (always on the receiving end of the kicks) and bow tie, declaiming about some outrageous trick he intends to play on his form master. Mr Quelch is sure to be hovering around, hearing every word Bunter is saying. It is Bunter, with his sublime ignorance both in education and in sport, his constant thefts of food, his transparent lies, and his postal order which never arrives, who can take the credit or blame for liberating *The Magnet* from the constricted public-school story code of Talbot Baines Reed and *The Boy's Own Paper*.

Even without Bunter there are times when it seems as if Greyfriars is nearer in spirit to Beachcomber's 'Narkover' and Jimmy Edwards's 'Chiselbury' than to St Dominic's. This does not, however, apply to the greatest dramatic series, like the two Wharton Rebel stories. Reading them after one of the more light-hearted stories is like visiting another age, as if a time machine had taken the reader from the 1930s into the 1880s.

But when Bunter is the featured star we are back in the moral climate of 'I'm all right, Jack'. Bunter never plays the game, and rarely gets his deserved punishment. There are whacks and canings galore (Greyfriars is not run on modern lines) but the impression never lasts longer than the next meal. His behaviour even swamps the other characters. Mr Quelch, normally a figure of stern authority, becomes in stories featuring Bunter the comedian's straight man. Even when expulsion threatens Bunter the subject is treated strictly for laughs. The fat owl actually prefers the sack to a flogging, and when the headmaster refuses to oblige he runs away, leaving the following letter:

ROTTERS!

I'm going.

I refuze to be phlogged, especially when I am innocent and it was only a joak all the time.

Yore a lott of unsimpathetic beests. I despize you!

Yours kontemptuously,

W. G. BUNTER

P.S.—I skorn the lott of you!

Perhaps the greatest set of stories featuring Billy Bunter was the Bunter Court series of 1925. Bunter Court did not exist except in Bunter's mind. Its real counterpart was Bunter Villa, a semi-detached house in the heart of Surrey commuterland. But in Bunter's imagination his home became a stately mansion with liveried servants and aristocratic guests.

How Bunter managed to transform this dream into reality

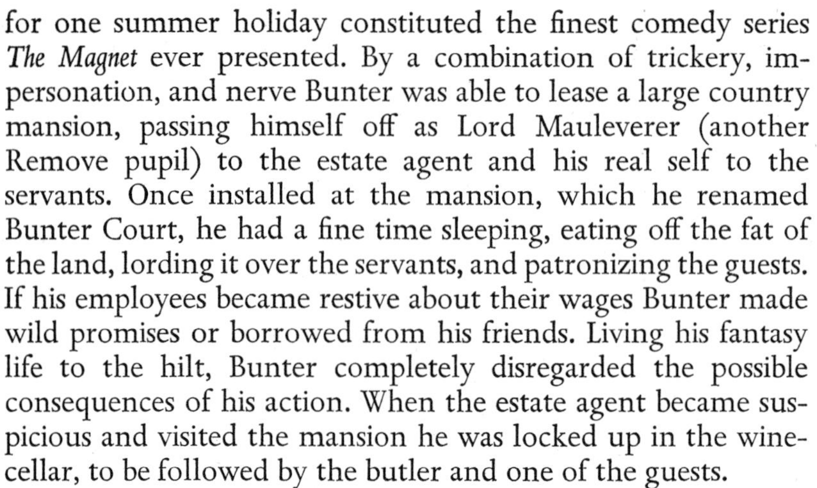

for one summer holiday constituted the finest comedy series *The Magnet* ever presented. By a combination of trickery, impersonation, and nerve Bunter was able to lease a large country mansion, passing himself off as Lord Mauleverer (another Remove pupil) to the estate agent and his real self to the servants. Once installed at the mansion, which he renamed Bunter Court, he had a fine time sleeping, eating off the fat of the land, lording it over the servants, and patronizing the guests. If his employees became restive about their wages Bunter made wild promises or borrowed from his friends. Living his fantasy life to the hilt, Bunter completely disregarded the possible consequences of his action. When the estate agent became suspicious and visited the mansion he was locked up in the wine-cellar, to be followed by the butler and one of the guests.

This series illustrates Bunter's redeeming trait, his contempt for authority in all its guises, coupled with a refusal to recognize his own modest place in society. Bunter is a Walter Mitty with the energy and nerve to bring his fantasies to life. In order to become a figure of authority himself, Bunter on various occasions impersonates a lord, a billionaire, and a circus proprietor, and the impersonations grow almost more real than his own identity. He is, of course, the victim of his own daydreams, believing that he has a fine figure, that he is kept out of the cricket and football teams through petty jealousy, and that if he put his mind to it he could be a first-class scholar.

Most young readers, however amusing they find Bunter, like to identify themselves with a true hero-figure, and Harry Wharton, captain of the Remove, had this role in *The Magnet*. But Wharton was a far from conventional hero. As well as being a born leader, with great potential for good, he was wilful, proud, hot-tempered, and quick to take offence. The 'Taming of Harry Wharton' was the theme of the first two stories ever to appear in *The Magnet*, but, like Bunter, he was not developed into a memorable character until the 1920s, when series, or serials, replaced single stories as the main fare of the paper.

In 1924–5 Wharton was featured in the first long series as the rebel of the form, at odds with his former friends and form master. The plot was melodramatic, but it was true tragedy in

the sense that Wharton's fall from grace was caused more by defects in his own character than through external misunderstandings. Anxious readers, not so used to long series at that date, sent many letters to the Amalgamated Press asking that Wharton should not be expelled. Three years later Wharton was again featured in a fine series, this time involving a personal feud set against a cricketing background.

Nearly half the stories which appeared in *The Magnet* in 1932 showed Wharton in some kind of trouble. In the first long series he lost the captaincy of the form to Vernon Smith, and later in the year he was again a rebel without a cause—some years before his time. Despite a contrived ending, this second Wharton Rebel series was much more skilfully written than the earlier set of stories, and showed how the author's style had developed over the years. The moral of a boy on the downgrade was not so strongly marked as before, but the razor-sharp description of Wharton's clashes with his form master are excellent. Anyone who thinks *The Magnet* is nothing but a collection of schoolboy japes and custard-pie humour should read this series.

But the most perfect 'Wharton in trouble' series came three years later, in 1935, when the *Magnet* stories generally were showing

traces of decline. Known as the 'Stacey series', it featured a relative and near-double who was determined to get Wharton expelled so that he could replace him in the affections of his uncle and guardian, Colonel Wharton. Needless to say, Stacey used his likeness to Wharton to good advantage.

The series is remarkable for its restrained adult atmosphere. Wharton never loses the support of his close friends, and he has other allies besides. Despite the many exciting will-he-get-out-of-it? situations the series can be read through without the desire to race to the end. The reason is that all the way through both rivals have their hours of triumph and tragedy. One of the best episodes describes how Wharton is forced to give up the captaincy of his form by Mr Quelch but manages to prevent

Stacey from being voted in his place. In passing it should be noted that Wharton's attitude towards his poor relation was far from charitable, even if his suspicions did prove to be justified.

The switch to *The Magnet* in 1926 came—luckily—when Hamilton was approaching his peak as a writer. Why a middle-aged author for boys who for decades had been turning out work of a consistently good but not exciting standard should be capable of this very definite improvement is something of a mystery. One can, however, point to Arthur Ransome and E. Nesbit who, like Hamilton, produced their best stories for juvenile readers in middle years and over a fairly limited period.

Hamilton was a brilliant scholar and translator (at one time he seriously considered a proposal to write boys' stories in French), and gifted enough as a musician and artist to want to make a career in these spheres. In the early years he might have had some regrets for giving up his time so whole-heartedly to writing mere boys' stories, but by the 1920s he was very proud of his work. Hamilton had a good idea of his own talent, even if his critics did not, and he was convinced that in his rather limited sphere of writing he was in a class of his own.

What should have been a great personal tragedy also contributed to the improvement in his work. Some time during the 1920s Charles Hamilton nearly went blind. This fortunately did not happen, but he remained extremely short-sighted for the rest of his life. One effect of this handicap was to put an end to his extensive European travels. His *Autobiography of Frank Richards* gives the impression that he was on a permanent Grand Tour of Europe before World War One. For the first time, he was able to settle down, and his enforced stability was of obvious help now that he was switching from complete stories to long series of 300,000 words or more.

Hamilton was obviously delighted that *The Magnet* was under his control again. The stories of the late 1920s have a gaiety and exuberance which are all the more endearing because they sometimes get out of hand. Who but Hamilton could make one half-believe that Billy Bunter, armed with stolen clothes, false moustaches, and beard, could pass himself off as a plump circus proprietor, while the real owner of the wigs goes about

unrecognized by his employees, except for a crooked manager who has his own reasons for letting the deception go on?

By the early 1930s *The Magnet* had reached full maturity. Hamilton was at the peak of his powers in stories—like the Brander rebellion series (1930), the Lancaster series (1931), second Wharton Rebel series (1932), and Stacey series (1935)—which combined logical and restrained plots with richer character drawing.

Charles Hamilton always enjoyed writing holiday stories. Foreign-travel series in particular were a regular feature of *The Magnet* in the 1920s and 1930s. His obvious pleasure was reflected in such series as the India series (1926), South Seas series (1927), Hollywood series (1929), China series (1930), and Kenya series (1931). It is significant that he retained most of these series when he handed in his *Magnets* and *Gems* for waste paper in the war.

Of these holiday stories probably only the China series is among the élite, but with their mixture of comedy and adventure or mystery they are perhaps more characteristic of Hamilton than the high farce of Bunter Court or the sustained dramatics of the best Wharton-in-trouble series.

Hamilton also had a flair for writing Christmas series combining just the right amount of comedy and mystery, usually of the haunted-house variety. Bunter was well to the fore in all these tales, the best probably being 'Cavandale Abbey' (1930), 'Mauleverer Towers' (1931), 'Wharton Lodge' (1933), 'Polpelly' (1935), and 'Reynham Castle' (1937).

Paradoxically a decline was now becoming evident in the less notable series of the same period. Richer characterization and better descriptive writing and narration did not always make up for repetitive plots, obvious padding, and a certain tiredness. Some of the very long series of the 1930s also outstayed their welcome. By 1935 a logical storyline for each series was largely being abandoned in favour of what might be termed episodic development. Each instalment tended to become more or less complete in itself despite its connection with other stories in the same series. For example, each issue of the Carter series (1938) shows how the new pupil tries to get Bunter expelled and fails. Luckily the series is more important as a vehicle for Billy Bunter than as a tale of suspense.

But this type of episodic storytelling had its dangers and was probably the key to the decline of *The Magnet*. A number of the later series are very good, but each achievement is something of a *tour de force* in the face of undistinguished plot construction.

In creating the world of *The Magnet* Hamilton owed a debt to two artists in particular, the late Leonard Shields, and Mr C. H. Chapman, who still illustrates the Bunter books. Both showed great understanding in bringing the Greyfriars scene to life. Shields perhaps looms the larger, if only because he did most of the illustrations for *The Magnet* in its peak years. His cover illustrations are distinctive and have a charming vintage quality.

Because Charles Hamilton wrote for so much of his career for ephemeral boys' papers his best work is in danger of being forgotten except among specialist collectors. This is unfortunate, because in *The Magnet* Hamilton created a world of magical charm, and even the best of the post-war Bunter books are no substitute for the earlier Greyfriars stories. Is it too much to hope that one day an enterprising publisher will reissue some of the old series unabridged and with the original illustrations so that a new generation can discover the treasure-house of stories now lying in the fading pages of *The Magnet*?

FIRE! FIRE!

Fire protection implements, 1556

THE SOCIAL HISTORY

OF THE FIRE BRIGADE BY

 AMORET AND CHRISTOPHER SCOTT 

EARLY man must have watched his most dangerous enemy rampaging through the forests with all the fear and hatred that come from a total inability to do anything about it. For fire-fighting needs organization and discipline, two characteristics notably lacking in the ancient world until the Romans civilized themselves.

In 300 B.C. there was a drilled body of municipal slaves, known as the *familia publica*, which was moderately active but not conspicuously successful in dealing with the fires which threatened with monotonous regularity to raze Rome to the ground. More active, but even less efficient, was the fire brigade which Crassus (the rich one) maintained some two hundred years later. Crassus's wealth derived largely from speculative enterprises, chief among which was the buying and selling of property. If a building in Rome caught fire his carefully trained firemen would dash to the scene and make great play with buckets, hooks, siphons, and vinegar-soaked blankets, successfully obstructing the municipal brigade until the house had burned to the ground. Crassus himself would then arrive and buy the desolated site from the dazed owner at a knock-down price. The word 'arson' was never actually spoken aloud in his presence. He eventually met his death at the hands of a Parthian general who with barbaric justice poured molten gold down Crassus's throat.

Fire brigades on the Roman pattern certainly came to Britain, but they disappeared with every other trace of civilization when the Romans left. Through the early centuries and the Middle Ages fires were regarded as Acts of God, and it was logically assumed that only another Act could stop them. To encourage this, the bones of a saint would be carried in procession round the burning building and the church bells rung in a reverse peal. Special fire-bells were cast for use impartially against thunder and lightning as well as mundane fires. Not everyone believed, however, that the ringing of bells could put a fire out. The Spaniards, hearing with satisfied horror of the Great Fire of London in 1666, were firmly convinced that the ringing of heretic bells had only served to make matters worse. There were unexpected social factors involved in the *source* of fires at about this time, too, if the recently ousted Royalists were to be believed. They swore that the disastrous fire which swept through Marlborough in 1653, after Cromwell had come to power, had been caused by 'his red and fiery nose, and was an ominous commencement of this incendiary's usurpation'.

The threat of fire in the towns of seventeenth-century England was a fearful one. In spite of ordinances to the contrary, houses were still built much as they had been five hundred years before, with the tightly packed timber frames leaning out towards each other over the narrow refuse-choked streets, and a sprinkling of thatched roofs to make the possibility of serious fires into a certainty. One after the other the major cities of the country caught fire and were rebuilt, often to burn again within a decade. Even in progressive Cromwellian London the sole source of water for fighting fires was the springs, reinforced by those few public-spirited householders who obeyed one of the face-saving ordinances of the City Fathers and kept a barrel of water ready filled in front of the house. When a fire began the neighbours formed a double chain from the nearest spring or barrel, men on one side, women on the other. Full buckets, as many as could be found, went up the men's side, empty ones down the women's.

By the middle of the seventeenth century fire-fighting equipment had almost reached the stage achieved by the Romans a millennium and a half before. 'Fire squirts' (brass hand-syringes), 'great squirts' (the same but larger, and held by two men while a third pushed the handle in and out), and the first primitive wheeled fire engines had all made their appearance. In addition, some civic authorities, led by London, were laying down and enforcing rules for the building of premises to minimize the dangers of fire.

The first underground water mains were a source of considerable expense to the municipalities that installed them. The only way of reaching the water when a fire broke out was to dig down into the street, find the hollowed-out log pipe and cut it open. The buckets and squirts were filled, the cisterns of the engines topped up, and the water then left to run out of the broken pipe until such time as the magistrates found the opportunity to have it replaced.

The Great Fire of London, which began in an Eastcheap baker's shop in the small hours of one Sunday morning in September 1666, was fought with this equipment, augmented by a good deal of gunpowder for making 'fire breaks' among buildings in the path of the flames. Fire-fighting in the City was the responsibility of the Lord Mayor, Sir Thomas Bludworth, who, summoned at three o'clock in the morning, took one sour look at the burning slum, said: 'Pish, a woman might piss it out,' and went back to bed. Four days later, in spite of the personal intervention of King Charles with a bucket, five-sixths of the City had been destroyed. The most astonishing feature of the whole tragic affair was that only six people died as a result of the holocaust.

The two important results from the Great Fire were the rebuilding of London in the form we know it today; and the formation in 1680 of the first of the fire-insurance companies (known as 'The Insurance Office at the Backside of the Royal Exchange') which were to play such a large part in the history of fire-fighting for the next three centuries. The idea spread rapidly, and new fire-insurance companies sprang up by the dozen in the course of the next fifty years, each with its own brigade and its own lead fire-mark, which was fixed to the outside of an insured house to show any other insurance company's brigade that happened on the scene that it could with righteous scorn watch the house and its occupants burn to death.

Quite the most attractive features of the uninhibited brigades which each of the insurance companies set up were the uniforms. The Hand-in-Hand brigade wore yellow plush breeches, a blue coat with silver buttons, and silver-buckled shoes; the Westminster men were dressed in blue coats and waistcoats embroidered with yellow, and black breeches worn with white stockings gartered in yellow. Underneath the gaudy impractical uniforms, which were entirely designed for advertisement, the members of the brigade (often recruited from among the Thames watermen) were tough. They needed to be. The hazards of actually fighting fires were slight compared with the other risks they ran.

There was the most murderous rivalry between the companies to get their own brigade to the scene of the fire first; and the monetary incentives offered (including the large sum of thirty shillings for the first engine to arrive) made sure that the men left their scruples behind when the bells rang out. Sabotage of a rival's equipment and running fights between brigades were commonplace, and if three or four companies arrived at the fire together it was almost certain that the blaze would rage unchecked until such time as the brigades had settled their differences.

The eighteenth-century engines were elementary structures. The water was still pumped from a cistern which was filled by relays of buckets from the nearest water source. The pumping power was purely manual and was transmitted by means of long handles running the length of the engine on each side. There were never enough men in the crew to work these handles, and relays of helpers were taken on from the crowd of onlookers.

As the usual payment for such help was a shilling and large quantities of free beer, there was no shortage of volunteers; the rush was so great that the firemen were often literally overwhelmed, and on more than one occasion the handles were seized and pumped up and down with such force that the engine was wrecked. If the regular firemen could fight off the eager surplus volunteers and get the engine going the handles would swing up and down to a chant, from forty dry throats, of 'Beer Oh! Beer Oh!'; and if beer was not produced the pumping stopped and the cry changed to 'No beer, no water'. Some brigades issued tokens to the volunteer pumpers which could be exchanged at their parent insurance offices for a shilling.

A landmark in the history of the fire brigade was the engine invented by Richard Newsham (a pearl-button maker) and patented in 1721. This machine, with its double cylinder and air-chamber, produced a continuous stream of water instead of the intermittent dribbles of the earlier models. Its fame spread across the Atlantic, and in 1731 the Common Councillors of New York resolved to buy two of them—the first fire engines in the country. Six months later Newsham's machines arrived; three days after they were unloaded they were in action.

Perhaps as a result of this auspicious start the volunteer fire brigades of New York developed a sentimental regard for their engines which lasted with undiminished fervour until the hand-engine gave way to the steamer in 1865. The earlier American engines were unlikely enough objects of love. Newsham's engine was commonly known as 'the bed poster', and it was indeed the nearest thing to a four-poster on wheels that had been seen outside a carnival. Its immediate successors, American built, followed much the same functional and angular pattern. But the shape of things to come was seen in the first successful engine produced in America; Thomas Lote's masterpiece modelled in 1743 on Newsham's was affectionately known as 'Old Brass Backs', from the prodigal use of brass fittings and ornaments.

The fierce pride of the New York brigades in their engines was very largely the result of the men being volunteers and not hired employees. The London insurance offices lavished money on splendid uniforms for their men to attract business; the men wore them and did their job because they were paid to. In New York to be a member of one of the city's brigades was a privilege; the engine was treated with the reverence accorded to the flag of a select regiment, and the most fitting way to do it honour was to decorate it.

The city authorities, who supplied the machine, sensibly realized that whatever colour they painted it on delivery, the particular fire company that got her (American fire engines were, and are, always female) would immediately change it. So the custom developed of supplying the engine finished in one coat of flat paint of some nondescript shade and letting the fire company go on from there. The members of the company happily dug deep into their often capacious pockets, and the results were the wonder of New York. One of the earliest decorated engines was Old Wreath of Roses, No. 15 Company's pride in 1796; she boasted several exquisite paintings of roses on her back and side panels.

As the years went by the modest embellishments of this engine began to look positively drab in comparison with some of the later fire engines of the city. In 1830 the members of No. 13 Company paid, from their own pockets, $800 to have the brass fittings of their machine silver-plated; engine No. 31 was rolled out one morning with solid gold figures let into its wooden sides. In 1849 the engine of No. 4 Company was re-decorated with a shining white box picked out in gold, blue and gold wheels, blue levers, a profusion of carved work inlaid with solid gold, and four large views of Niagara Falls painted on mahogany panels fixed to the sides.

The engines were christened with great ceremony and given stirring names—Lafayette, Hudson, Fulton—when they were first put into commission, but they were soon given other less formal names by the outside world: Old Blue Box, Man-killer (which had stiff pumping-handles), Big Six, White Ghost, The Arsenal (generally thought to be kept filled with revolvers when not in action), and so on.

It was more than likely that The Arsenal was indeed full of revolvers, and probably cutlasses, shot-guns, and dynamite as well. The rivalry between the various companies was fanatical, and the tenderest spot at which to aim was the sacred engine. Nineteenth-century New York was entertained, and occasionally terrified, by a series of the most magnificent actions, ranging from fireside brawls to full pitched battles, between fire companies avenging the besmirched honour of their beloved machines. In 1843 the crew of the Black Joke engine, No. 33, defended their station against several hundred firemen from other companies with a howitzer loaded to the muzzle with chains and bolts.

Another fruitful source of conflict between the companies was the race to get the hose connected to the widely spaced fire hydrants which had been built into the street mains. Most companies had a hand-picked advance guard of roughnecks at constant readiness in the station, whose sole job it was to rush out when the alarm reached the station, capture the nearest hydrant to the fire, and hold it against all other companies until their own engine arrived. One company is recorded as having fought for two hours with another for possession of a cannon-muzzle buried in the street, which both sides thought was a hydrant. Another company, scorning the use of bullies, would send off at the first alarm an elegantly dressed gentleman carrying a barrel. On arrival at the fire, he would slip his barrel over the nearest hydrant, and sit nonchalantly on it until his engine arrived, smoking a cigar while the rival companies desperately searched for the source of water.

The greatest indignity that could befall an engine was the dreaded 'washing', in which one engine pumped so hard that water was forced back down the main into another engine, which overflowed. The disgrace was not so much the disparaging comparisons between the power of the crews manning the washer and the washed, as the dreadful effect the overflowing water had on the decorations of the engines. A 'washed' engine was often artistically ruined, and therefore unable to appear.

At the time that New York was disbanding its volunteer

brigades, in 1865, London was muddling along with its fire-fighting through a maze of self-sown obstacles. There were eight quite distinct water companies in the City; some had hydrants fitted in their mains, some had none. Hoses which fitted one hydrant would not fit another. Only in a few parts was there a continuous supply of water, while elsewhere the brigade was powerless until the turncock had been fetched. In 1866 the London Fire Engine Establishment (an amalgamation of the insurance companies who founded the first brigades) was taken over by the City, and the Metropolitan Fire Brigade was founded, under the redoubtable figure of Captain Shaw, who was regarded by the public as the personification of all firemen heroes, past, present, and future.

If London's organization was muddled the situation in some of the other towns of England, and in the country districts, was chaotic. Nearly two hundred years after an ordinance of 1707 had laid down the rules country parishes still found their feelings divided between the onerous burden of maintaining a hand-pump, as the law required (when there were perfectly efficient insurance brigades which could do the job a great deal better), and the desire for the rewards which the same Act promised for the first, second, and third engines to arrive at a fire. In Birmingham the municipal authorities observed the letter of the law by keeping an ancient bed-poster under the command of one of the street scavengers, who would stagger into sight dragging his disreputable machine some half an hour after the flamboyant insurance brigades had galloped their horse-drawn engines into action.

The difficulty of fixing the responsibility for fire-fighting on any particular organization was further complicated in the nineteenth century by the presence of volunteer brigades in the New York pattern, works brigades, and private brigades. Frederick Hodges, who owned a distillery in Lambeth, founded in 1851 one of the most famous and efficient of the works brigades. His original intention was not philanthropy but the protection of his highly inflammable distillery. However, his two large manual engines were soon attending fires all over London, often beating the London Fire Engine Establishment machines into third place. The volunteer brigades of the 1870s relied heavily on subscription and money-raising efforts to pay for the latest equipment, which they felt compelled to buy in order to avoid being outshone by more affluent rival brigades; and their financial difficulties were aggravated by the general replacement at about this time of the old manual pump by the expensive steamer.

Quite the most gorgeously equipped fire organizations of the nineteenth century were the 'country-house' brigades, founded for the same reasons that led to the other unofficial fire-fighters —the inability, or wilful refusal, of the parishes to do the job themselves. Although their primary purpose was to protect the manor and the estate surrounding it, the country-house engines, drawn by superb horses and often captained by the noble lord himself in a Ruritanian uniform, would very often attend fires at some distance for the sake of experience. When the village of Eynsham was burned in 1854 there was a gathering of brigades from Blenheim Palace, Wytham Abbey, Cokethorpe Park, Oxford University, and even the University Press.

The unromantic twentieth century took most of the beauty out of the fire brigade. Scientific advances and stodgy Acts of Parliament succeeded one another to take away the belching steamer, the horses (one of the first motor-driven engines was tried out in 1902 by the Liverpool brigade; its unreliable ignition system propelled it in a series of explosive jerks, and the machine was generally known as Farting Annie), the gaudy uniforms. But while the romance was being squeezed out the fresh air of efficiency was rushing in. It was not until the Second World War was over, however, that the National Fire Service was fully organized in Britain, and it took the two terrible months of September and October 1940, when the bombs fell on London every night without a break, for the British public to realize just what it owes to its firemen.

SF Art

SCIENCE FICTION COVERS UNCOVERED

BRIAN W. ALDISS

THIS YEAR has seen a revolutionary change in science fiction publishing, with the magazines which have for so long been a colourful part of the genre's background fighting a losing battle against a changing environment. In the main they are vanishing unwept; but to a small group of devotees and eccentrics an epoch is nearly over, and that is always worth commemorating.

The epoch began in 1926, when the first magazine to be devoted entirely to science fiction, *Amazing Stories*, was published in New York. The editor was Hugo Gernsback, the publisher to the Experimental Publisher Company Inc. Certainly the experiment was a success. *Amazing* is still published today, despite many vicissitudes, while the 'Hugo'—a large and splendidly phallic spaceship—is the most coveted annual prize in the world of SF.

Looking back at some of those early issues, turning the pages carefully, for they are yellowed and crack easily, I pause at the quaint old device that stands at the head of the title page. It is labelled 'Jules Verne's Tombstone at Amiens Portraying his Immortality', and shows Verne, full of post-mortemnal exuberance, lifting the stone lid of his coffin and offering a greeting to the world, his hand extended.

Such grand gestures—particularly such grand gestures from unlikely places—were then and are still typical of science fiction. And the gestures have spilled over on to the covers of the magazines.

On the covers you will find the heroes defying a horde of antmen, or the great spaceships with all their lights ablaze as they plunge into a giant sun, or the damsels in the best-fitting space suits, or the mightiest machines, or the most Jurassically inclined animals, or the rudest robots with the shapeliest girls on their shoulders as they head towards what impossible miscegenation.

One cover from 1929, on a *Science Wonder Stories*, shows the predecessor of all flying saucers snatching away into space a skyscraper that I, in my British ignorance, have always thought of as the Woolwich Building. Another saucer behind it makes good time into the infinite with the Eiffel Tower. The editor offered a prize for the best story written round this cover. His second rule governing the competition was that the story 'should be plausible in the light of our present knowledge of science'.

This note of seriousness was prevalent in the early days, from the covers, through the stories, to the correspondence columns at the back, which were printed in miniscule print and carried letters on which were bestowed such titles as 'Good Wishes and A Kindly Criticism from a Lady'.

SF has rarely received much kindly criticism from ladies. At first it was too plodding and scientific for them; stories were introduced with such forbidding announcements as '[the author] has had the collaboration of the most famous German scientists'.

Later, especially during the 'thirties, SF became too full of horror for the gentler sex.

Incidentally, although the Anglo-Saxon races seem still to be the only ones who can write tolerable SF (with the solitary and doubtful exception of Jules Verne), a strong Germanic influence was evident in the early days of SF magazines. The first issue of *Thrilling Wonder Stories*, in the mid-'thirties, featured such exotic names as Weinbaum, Zagat, Ernst, and Otis Adelbert Kline.

The covers of the 'thirties, at their most typical, showed scenes of destruction or potential destruction. A fine example is the cover of *Fantasy*, a brief-lived British magazine that was an early casualty of the war. It depicts giant caterpillars stopping the roar of London's traffic while the fire brigade souses them with plaster of Paris (within a year London's fire brigades were more desperately engaged in real life). Mighty interstellar moths had been attracted across the gulfs of space towards the lights of Earth, and there had laid their eggs.

Unfeasible though this idea is, it has the immediate poetic appeal that is found in the best SF, and transcends purely scientific considerations. This horror phase of SF did have virtue in that it taught its writers not to plod as they had done earlier. The cover artists, too, began to learn, and to be known; by 1936 *Wonder Stories* could boast of a 'Cover in oils by the world-famous Paul'. Connoisseurs who still treasure sets and runs of these old magazines distinguish between Frank R. Paul's pink and blue periods.

Like many of his contemporaries Paul was fond of what may be termed the 'fearful odds' cover, with various unlucky space-going types besieged and outnumbered by creatures from the plutonian depths or savage sword-men from Saturn. Another favourite subject for pictorial representation was one monstrous and generally scaly carnivore demolishing the rocket that holds Our Hero's only hope of return to Earth, while Our Hero himself stands fast in the foreground, hopefully shooting out eyes with a sporting rifle. Fortunately this essay is no place in which to discuss the inner significance of some of these visions.

After Paul, perhaps Wesso, Morey, and Schneeman were the

best-known artists of the day. Wesso painted some captivating astronomical covers—a theme that has always been a safe bet for SF magazine editors wishing to avoid the worst of the horrors.

With the 'forties, and the war, the era of titles like 'Moon of Mad Atavism' was threatened. A more intelligent type of story, fast-moving but logical, made its appearance—notably in *Astounding*, for so long the best of all the magazines, the one with the most devoted audience, and the one to feature the SF writers best known today: Asimov, Heinlein, Simak, Clement, van Vogt, Anderson, Russell, Clarke, and so on. Their stories, particularly serials such as Kuttner's 'Fury', and E. E. Smith's 'Lensman' series, were the occasion for really imposing work by cover artists like Rogers and Timmins. For the first time, covers with atmosphere and dimension were appearing.

Two long decades later I find it hard to convey the in-group feeling (as we would now call it) that came from reading the 'forties SF magazines, particularly in Britain, where they could be obtained only with difficulty and then perhaps in some back-street tobacconist's and newsagent's.

How many times did I ask: 'Have you an *Astounding*, please?' to be met with a raised eyebrow and the question: 'An astounding what?' Those men knew not that they sold something beyond price.

Much of the in-group feeling was engendered because parents and schoolmasters and other powerful entities were against SF; they *knew*, just by looking at the magazine covers, that the contents were worthless.

But a change was coming. The readers, pitched into a world war, were growing up; and the war itself became more and more like science fiction. When the A-bomb was dropped on Hiroshima it was *Astounding* that gave me the first intelligible account of its working. For the first time I realized that the agreeable stuff I had been reading bore a valuable relationship to the real world: SF, after all, had predicted the atom bomb for many a year.

A lot of people must have come to the same realization about the validity of SF as I did. It became immensely popular. A boom was on! In the early 'fifties there were suddenly dozens of SF magazines. Even in Britain their bright covers could be seen throughout the land, and every W. H. Smith's was a joy.

The contents of many of these magazines were singularly disappointing. Too many markets were chasing too few writers, with the inescapable result that hacks from other fields who did not know a chromosome from a chronometer moved in and began to rewrite their old stories, this time setting them on Mars.

But the infusion of new blood was not all bad. Some of the new magazines brought a genuinely new approach to SF, and still survive today, while their more anaemic brethren are forgotten. Such survivors are *Galaxy*, *The Magazine of Fantasy and Science Fiction*, and *If*.

The last-named in particular featured some unusual covers by Ken Fagg, who showed a fine colour sense most artists before him had lacked. At this time, in the early 'fifties, new writers who were to prove their worth and stay to contribute good things, men like Philip K. Dick, Fred Pohl, and Damon Knight, were making themselves known. So was one of the most pleasing of all cover artists, the man who signs himself 'Emsh'.

Ed Emshwiller is enormously productive. Despite occasional lapses of taste, however, he has introduced a note new to SF coverage—a note of joy, which is present even in his more sinister work, masked as glee or disguised as swagger.

Sex has played a small part on SF covers, although generally in a purely conventional role. SF has never really had much time for women, and the covers have invariably shown her—when they showed her at all—as the potential victim of a fate more lurid than death: menaced by fantastic beasts, carted away by green men, anaesthetized in alien operating theatres, chased by metal menaces of her virtue. Where her role was not entirely passive, her one activity was to scream.

Emsh changed that. His women bound about strange planets, lightly clad, happy, unafraid; or they wear spikes and carry daggers, or beckon poor spacemen on from lonely eminences. For my vote, Emsh has done SF cover art a power of good; and the same must be said for his delightful wife and model, Carol.

Others have taken heart from Emsh's example. Despite a

penchant for depicting himself, the Irishman Gerard Quinn executed some light-hearted and appealing covers. Kirby did some fine fantasy covers for *Authentic*, and can now sometimes be found on the front of SF paperbacks. In a more serious vein Schoenherr does very professional work for *Analog*. Cover design has improved at the same time, while those flaming words 'Amazing', 'Fantastic', 'Stupefying', and so on, have reluctantly come to heel and retreated into a neat logotype at the top of the page.

Perhaps the best examples of co-operation between artist and editor were afforded in the late 'fifties by *New Worlds* and *Science Fantasy*, both edited by the man who for so long has been the centre of British SF, John (Ted) Carnell. With his artist, Brian Lewis, he produced a series of neat covers on both his magazines, where contemporary or futuristic shapes straggled across surrealist landscapes. Great promise lay in this line of experiment; although it was dropped before it had gone far enough, those few covers remain unique.

It is significant that this is as far as any magazine has gone towards abstraction. By and large, for all their supposed revolutionary content, they have been ultra-conservative in manner and hold firmly to representation at a rather literal level. This fear of what the cash customer (and particularly the ex-customer!) will think is entirely understandable to anyone familiar with the hazards of publishing. But it explains why at their worst the SF covers are abominable and at their best merely curious or charming.

An exception might perhaps be made for Chesley Bonestell, whose *trompe l'œil* scenes of men and spaceships on other planets were unprecedented for accuracy; but he was not a cover artist as such, and has since passed on to scene-designing for the cinema.

Since SF is a literature of change, it is fitting that it should itself be constantly undergoing change. The most obvious example of this is the weather-vane of *Astounding*'s name. Beginning as an imitator of Gernsback's *Amazing*, it was called ASTOUNDING *Stories* at first, and then, in turn, ASTOUNDING *Science Fiction*, *Astounding* SCIENCE FICTION, ASTOUNDING SCIENCE FICTION (with many subtle variations in print size of all the component words), ASTOUNDING *Analog Science Fact and Fiction, Astounding* ANALOG *Science Fact and Fiction*, and now sails serenely on as a Condé Nast publication officially called ANALOG *Science Fact* ⟶ *Science Fiction.* The hieroglyph apparently stands for 'transforming into'.

But whatever hoops *Analog* jumps through, and whatever vicissitudes face the other magazines, deeper changes continue remorselessly. Since the war the immense swing towards paperbacks has meant a swing away from magazine fiction. Paperbacks are the fashion; magazines, by and large, are not. This is why, although the SF-reading public continues to expand, the magazines that were SF's sole nursery (and one uses the term advisedly) are shrinking. Their main labours are over.

By saying this I am not forgetting that the work of H. G. Wells and his contemporaries, such as William Hope Hodgson, Conan Doyle, and Olaf Stapledon, was not written to appear in SF magazines. But the fact is that our diet of SF in the 'sixties owes more to the magazines than to Wells—although Wells had an influence over the magazine writers: often to little effect.

Nowadays, the old covers, with their mighty white cities, impossible architecture, man-devouring forests, and other delectable props, are steam engines among the diesel traffic of paperbacks. Their days are numbered. But science fiction, which today reaches a wider and more critical audience than it ever did, goes on; and in another twenty years, in *Saturday Book 44*, someone else may be nostalgically recalling the glories and idiocies of paperback SF covers.

Someone else? Nonsense! I have plenty of material accumulating for that article already.

The illustration by J. Cawthorn reproduced on page 170 is a cover drawing for SCIENCE FANTASY, *1963.*

his was a large ($8\frac{1}{2} \times 11\frac{3}{4}$ inches) nd gaudy cover by perhaps the avourite of the old-time cover ainters, Paul. It appeared in 1929. wo decades later thousands of eople were claiming to see 'fly- ng saucers' much like the one aul depicted.

The Venusians, attempting to land in eastern Labrador, are seen off by a fine assortment of monoplanes and biplanes, with an airship thrown in for luck. Morey's cover on the first of all the science fiction magazines appeared in 1932.

This magazine appeared in 1939, only a short while before war broke out. Among the contributors—many of them still writing SF—are two who later became known under different names: Russell Fearn as Vargo Statten, and John Beynon as John Wyndham.

A wartime cover by Hubert Rogers. The rocketship launching ramps are beginning to disintegrate. A taste for the gigantic—inanimate or otherwise—has long characterized science fiction. But Hubert Rogers was also fond of drawing young children; when he put them on the covers readers objected. They paid their money, after all, for spaceships.

This is a Rogers of 1947 vintage. SF was then preoccupied with how atomic power could be controlled. This story, 'Fury', written by Henry Kuttner under one of his many pen-names, portrayed a future in which the world had been carelessly destroyed by atomic war; the surviving men lived in great 'keeps' under the seas of Venus.

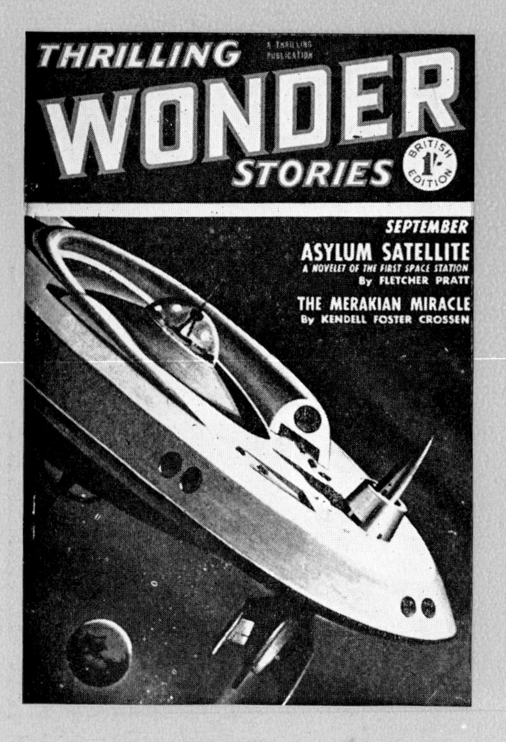

Above: an example of celestial architecture from a 1952 cover. This was a science fiction boom year. At that time people liked to read about man's first foray into space; editors were surprised to find that the first sputniks and satellites killed—rather than boosted—magazine sales.

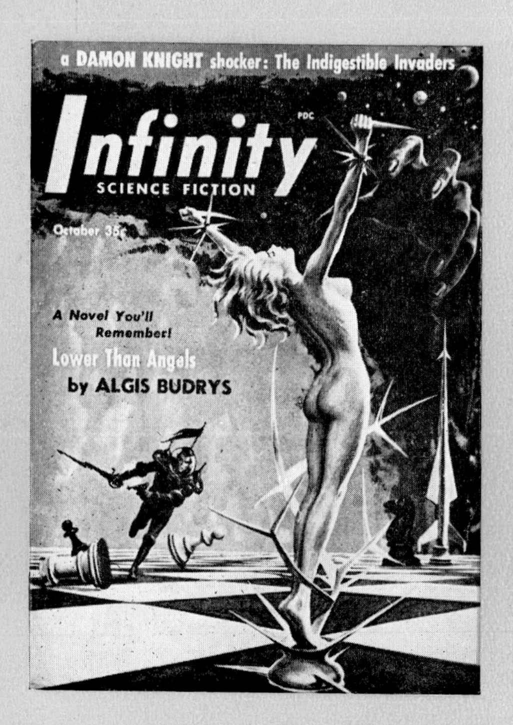

Amazing has undergone several reincarnations since its first appearance in 1928. From its 1953 style comes this cover by Clarence Doore, embodying in rather unexpected context the continued rivalry between man and machine.

On the left is one of Emsh's more symbolic covers, with well-armed knight charging across cosmic chessboard to rescue a lady who looks as if she will cause him a certain amount of trouble when he arrives. In the background: SF's most permanent and provocative symbol, the gleaming metal spaceship.

Ken Fagg executed a memorable series of covers for *If* in 1954. The one opposite was mainly in yellow, brown, and black, and depicts space-suited archaeologists exploring a site on an alien planet. Who knows what was Fagg's inspiration for the tower? A telephoto lens, perhaps?

if
WORLDS of SCIENCE FICTION
VOL. 1 No. 8.
Price 1/6

Neat layout is the rarest thing on a science fiction cover. Here it eclipses the artwork. The painting, by Brian Lewis, offers a pleasant contrast between the tumble-down shack and the condiment-containers, whole-heartedly Scandinavian in design. In its last few numbers, *Science Fantasy* reverted to non-pictorial covers. This issue appeared in 1959.

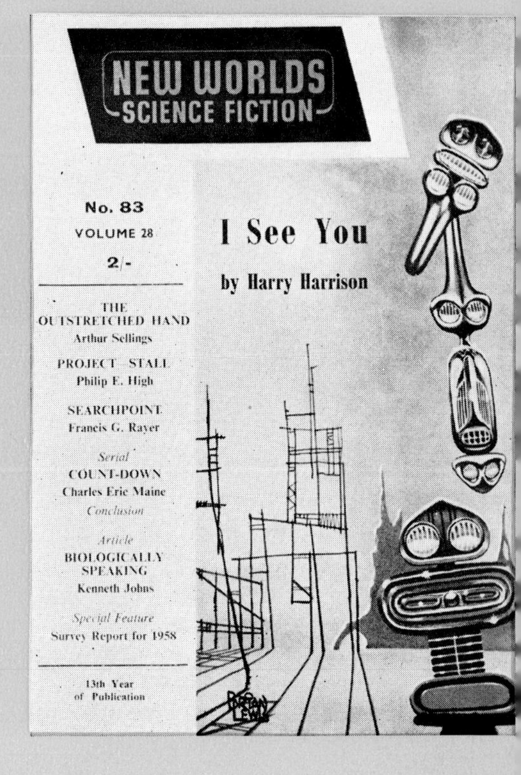

New Worlds was the sister magazine to *Science Fantasy*, and by common consent the best British magazine ever to appear. This example, from 1959, shows one of the most intriguing of Brian Lewis's semi-surrealist covers, with decorative shapes taken from car lights, instruments, and radiators. *New Worlds* tried many cover styles; its experiments with informal photographs of its authors were also pleasing.

Virgil Finlay's flowing line used to appear in the old *Weird Stories* and other pulp magazines of the 'thirties. This decorative cover was his work, and appeared in 1962. *Galaxy* arrived in the SF boom years when many of its competitors were so short-lived, and has proved its staying power. Hypnotic covers like this may be part of the answer.

Egyptian

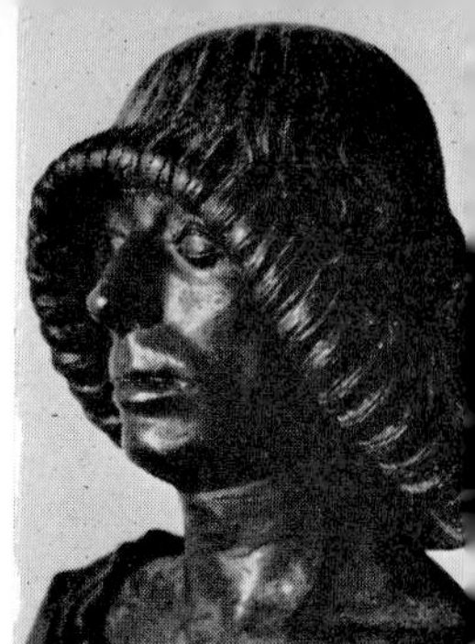

Renaissance

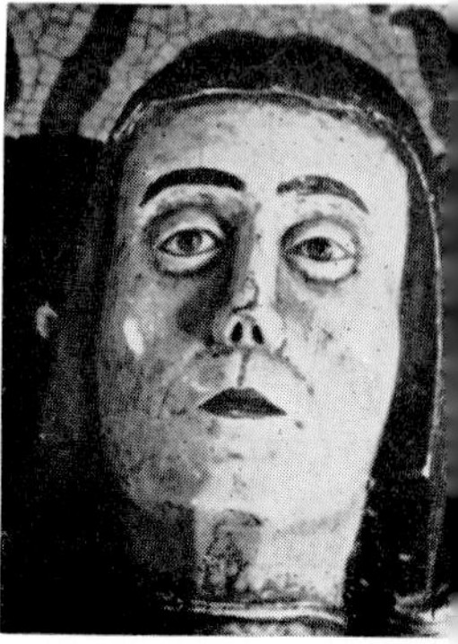

Medieval

Etruscan

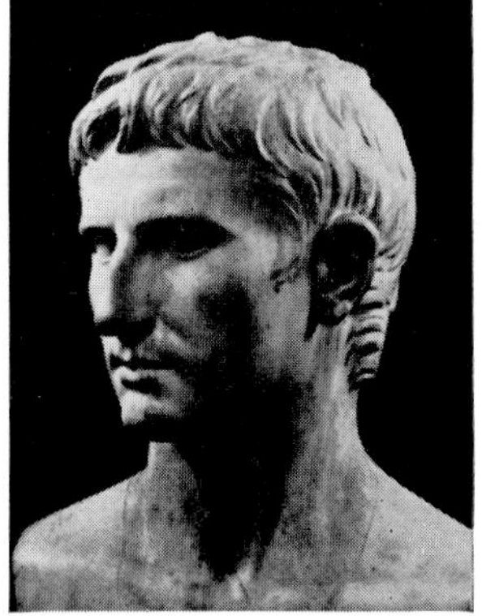

Roman (Augustus)

Above: Buddhist

Below: Greek

Below: Merovingia

Get Your Hair Cut!

OLIVE COOK

IN THE twentieth century men have been apt to regard long hair or any sign of vanity in its arrangement as a symptom of effeminacy. 'Get your hair cut!' is a traditional objurgation of the army sergeant-major. The hair of the respectable citizen must be close-cut, parted on the left or right and smoothly combed either to the side or straight back. A head cropped in the style forced upon Van Gogh by illness denotes masculinity beyond reproach. Yet men of other ages have rejoiced in luxuriant, decorative tresses as outward tokens of their virility. No one ever levelled the charge of unmanliness against the heroes of the Homeric period because they went into battle with stiff round curls in a scallop edge about their foreheads, with side ringlets and with a mane of snake-like locks hanging down behind their ears. Chaucer's young squire with 'lokkes crulle as they were leyd in presse' was the embodiment of a lusty lover. The gallantry of Pepys, who rushed to buy two voluminous periwigs, one for £3 and another for forty shillings, the moment the fashion came in, has never been questioned.

In the past a shorn head has usually stood for loss of power or for some other calamity. The Greeks cut their hair short for mourning. To the Merovingian kings a shaven head marked the end both of royal and manly power. Even as late as the first half of the seventeenth century a short style, with the hair brushed forward from the sides over the temples, was considered appropriate only for an ageing man.

The Roman attitude to long hair is something of an exception. Just as the Romans at the height of their power, unlike the men of all races and periods other than our own, despised any garment more ostentatious than the austere and spotless toga, so they affected a trimmed head and only permitted their locks to grow as a sign of grief. But who can fail to remark the resemblance between the cut of Augustus's noble ringlets and that adopted by the Beatles in 1964? The Emperor's hair falls in just the same soft line low on the nape of the neck and sweeps forward from the crown into just such a full fringe. The all-important difference is one of age and status. No self-respecting professional man or official of Augustus's years would dare today to make a public appearance with such a hair-do; it would label him at once as spiv, artist, or something more degenerate.

The originator of the Roman mode is said to have been Julius Caesar, who cut his hair and wore a laurel wreath to conceal his increasing baldness. Whether this be true or not the fashion exhibits a spirit of independence from tradition which encouraged the leaders of the First Republic under Napoleon to copy their coiffure from the portrait busts of Roman emperors. The style was comparatively short-lived and the defeat of Bonaparte and a return to a more familiar if unsettled order was accompanied by freely flowing tresses.

Hannibal, we are told, possessed two wigs, one to intensify his masculine beauty, the other to render him unrecognizable among his troops. In civilizations such as that of ancient Egypt, which were dominated by resistance to change, the wig was indispensable. It was made of real hair or of wool, according to a man's standing, was dyed jet black and was worn to the shoulders with a fringe in front. The fashion continued unaltered for centuries.

The wearing of wigs was vehemently denounced by the leaders of the early Christian Church. St Clement of Alexandria was horrified by the thought that a Christian might be wearing the hair of an infidel even then burning in hell and stated that it was 'a most sacrilegious thing for spurious hair to shade the head, covering the skull with dead locks. For on whom does the Presbyter lay his hand?' St Clement obviously felt that the Benediction was unable to pass through a wig to its wearer. Nevertheless bishops of the Church of England were adorned with wigs at the wedding of Queen Victoria, and the wig was an essential part of a gentleman's attire throughout the whole of Christian Europe for nearly a century and a half from about 1660. The peruke was raised to a fine art by Louis XIV who employed as many as forty perruquiers at Versailles, giving them the official title of artists. Although already over six feet tall, Louis adopted the wig to make himself yet more imposing.

When the huge full-bottomed wig first came in, it was composed of natural coloured hair. It could not be too big, for its size was a gauge of social eligibility. The public combing of this mass of false hair with a jewel-set ivory comb became a modish London pastime to be observed daily in the Mall, the theatre box, or drawing-room.

The powder closets found in eighteenth-century houses testify to the strange, irrational custom of coating the wig or the natural hair with finely ground clay or with flour to which the vogue for white hair, inaugurated by Louis XIV in old age, led. The powdering process had to be endured at least twice and, to be really elegant, thrice daily and a special room was found to be essential for the ritual whatever the method of application. Some men would stick their heads through a curtain during the operation to spare their coats, while others preferred to bury their faces in a glass funnel.

The fantastically exaggerated hair styles of women towards the close of the eighteenth century were accompanied by continual change in the modes for men. Now the wig was worn high and smooth in front; now it assumed the shape of a broken pediment; now the sides fluffed out like pigeon's wings; now they descended over the ears in horizontal rolls. Sometimes a pigtail, varying in length, hung down the middle of the back; sometimes it was twisted in loops. With the social upheaval at the end of the period wig and powder were flung aside in favour of short natural hair, except in the case of those for whom powdered hair was a demonstration of political principles, a noble aristocratic gesture against Whigs and Radicals.

It was not only at the time of the French Revolution that social change was accompanied by feverish variations in men's hair styles. Decadent Romans had recourse to coloured wigs of diverse and exotic aspect; and the XVIIIth Dynasty of the Egyptian civilization, when collapse was imminent, witnessed abrupt deviations from the traditional coiffure. Wigs became long and wavy, some terminated in corkscrew curls, others fell forward in rolls to well below the collar bone, and very often the wool or false hair was dyed bright red or blue.

Viewed in the perspective of these observations the swiftly

succeeding modes of our own period would seem to bode little good, though account must of course be taken of the fact that the conventionally cropped citizens who remain aloof from innovation are immensely more numerous than those Tories of the old school who were still going about with whitened hair as late as 1820. Nevertheless a bewildering variety of styles has been paraded by fashionable youths during the last decade. The crew cut (from the lumberjacks of Canada) has given way to subtle variations of the Duck's Anatomy, to the 'Dale Robertson', 'the Director' (slight wave on the crown), 'the Academician' (high side parting), 'the Author', 'the Olympic', 'the Continental', 'the Editor' (high side parting, both sides swept up with hair immediately above the ears going right back), and to American styles featuring a horizontal parting across the head from ear to ear. The social-snob names are in themselves symptomatic of instability.

Yet, whatever the socio-political implications, is the keen revival of male interest in hair arrangement truly a sign of unmanliness? There is no doubt that the interest exists, and not only in younger men. A report on 'National Hair and Beauty Week' published in the *Manchester Guardian* as long ago as 1956 informed us that 'some of the older men in the suburbs no longer seek a simple back and sides, but sit back for such improvements as permanent waving, silver and gilt threads and tipped gilt ends'. Dyeing, unknown for generations, is making a male comeback.

Is not this inclination for more ornamental styles, for artificial aid, a sign of revolt against the overlong and unnatural domination of the subdued and mouse-like close-shorn head, of revived faith in the Samson myth, of a general return to the colour and flamboyancy in which men delighted before the Machine Age? And may not the accusation of effeminacy merely result from the fact that modern woman has paraded her emancipation by aping so many masculine styles of all periods, including the straight bob and fringe of the late Middle Ages and the page-boy cut with rolled-under ends of the Renaissance, that it has become difficult to ascribe any fashion with certainty to man alone except that basic crop exemplified by Van Gogh?

The eighteenth-century full-bottomed wig

bove: Jacobean

Above: The Peruke

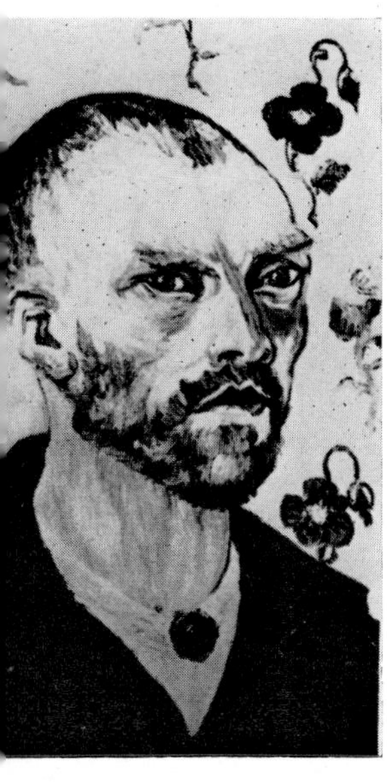

-portrait by Van Gogh

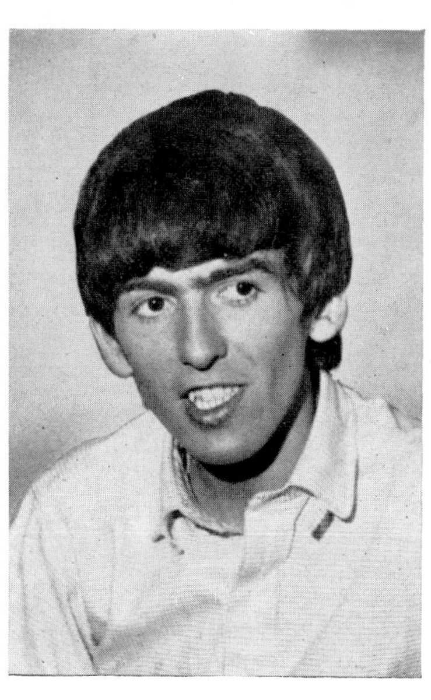

The Beatle style, 1964

The Romantic style, 1820

The Old School Tie —and all that

ANGUS McGILL

IT ALL started, so they say, at Oxford some time in the 1880s. One afternoon a rowing chap took the ribbon off his boater and put it round his neck. 'I say, dash it,' he said, 'I've invented the old school tie.'

Well, perhaps that's not *exactly* what he said, but it would have been the truth if he had. The idea was an immediate success. Soon every other rowing chap was wearing *his* boater ribbon as a tie to show that he was not only a rowing chap but that he was a member of a particular group of rowing chaps—a group from which lesser chaps were excluded.

This was intoxicating stuff for undergraduates—and for more than just them. The concept of an emblem exclusive to a group has always been irresistible to the English, and before long the club tie was spreading far beyond Oxford. Within a few years every school had its school tie and its old school tie, every college its college tie, every regiment its regimental tie. Ties multiplied wherever you looked. There were cricket club ties, shove-ha'penny club ties, county ties and town ties, firm's ties and profession ties. There is now a tie to fit almost any field of human endeavour. There is a nuclear physicist's tie. There is a tie exclusive to those who planned the Suez operation. Apparently they are proud of it! There is a Smithfield Meat Market tie.

---

posite, upper row, from left to right: M.C.C.; All England Lawn Tennis Club; London ottish Rugby Football Club; Harlequin Rugby Football Club; British Ski Club.

posite, lower row, from left to right: Royal Scots Greys; 10th Royal Hussars (Prince of ales' Own); 11th Hussars (Prince Albert's Own); Royal Gloucester Hussars; Fife and rfar Yeomanry.

Indeed at least thirty thousand different ties, all asserting exclusiveness, togetherness, and a comforting feeling of belonging, were born that far-off afternoon on the Isis.

The ties differ widely, but they can all be recognized on sight as being club ties of some kind. Generally speaking—*very* generally speaking—long-established organizations, which acquired a tie early, went in for stripes; those who came later prefer crests. The more recent the organization, the more curious the *motif*. There are now ties with ships on them, animals on them, sputniks on them. The Mini-Minor tie has little Mini-Minors. There isn't a Rolls-Royce tie, which is about the only thing that makes owners of Rolls-Royces feel under-privileged.

Crested ties can be registered and thus protected from any upstart organization that may be prowling about. Striped ties can't be registered. So if you really want your new Boozing, Wenching and Medieval Church Music Study Group to have a dark blue tie with a pale blue diagonal stripe, then I suppose you can. But Old Etonians hope you won't. That's *their* tie you're mucking about with.

The O.E. is the archetypal old school tie. It is, from many points of view, an enviable possession. It means, to begin with, that its wearer never starves. One governs in such a tie. One is on the Board. One gets a taxi immediately, while persons wearing other ties shout their heads off and get soaked in the rain.

A Guards tie also bestows a quiet, deep-rooted prestige, and, like the O.E., suggests iron-clad, gilt-edged credit. This is why these ties are so enduringly popular with the confidence trickster. Many is the impostor in the O.E. tie who has filched the odd fiver from the genuine O.E., many the bounder in the Guards tie who has asked for fifty-seven other offences to be taken into consideration.

Firms like C. H. Munday's, just off Leicester Square, who sell these ties, do their utmost to see that they go only round the right necks. But then any well-trained tie salesman can spot a rotter at fifty paces, and one who has a *real* feeling for an old school tie wouldn't dream of selling one to just anyone. The customer may bristle. The customer may glare. The customer *has* been known actually to bang the counter, which just shows how far some of these chaps will go. But no tie salesman worth his stripes is intimidated. If the gentleman didn't go to Rugby, then he can't have an Old Rugbeian tie, and that's that.

Still, it isn't a legal offence in Great Britain to wear any tie you choose to wear, unless, I suppose, you devise one that is noticeably pornographic. You can't even be prosecuted for wearing, without the due and complex preliminaries, an M.C.C. tie. In this, as in so much else, we are unlike South Africa. There they passed a law in 1935 forbidding citizens to behave in so caddish a manner. Anyone who does so can be arrested and, I suppose, fined. It is hard to believe, but then so much in that land today is hard to believe.

A curious thing about the old school tie is that shabbiness is a virtue. New-looking old school ties aren't at all the thing, and new old boys have been known to rough up their new old school ties before putting them on.

Perhaps the most popular club tie in England is the R.A.F. tie, which you see all over the place. I doubt whether the reason for this is wholly statistical. Perhaps the R.A.F., being the youngest of the fighting services, feels a keener urge to assert its identity. But then you see a lot of naval ties too. Fighting folk are obviously attracted to colours, badges, flags, and so forth.

But popularity isn't the point of ties at all. The more exclusive the tie the happier are its wearers. When too many people become entitled to a tie the group tends to splinter into smaller, more exclusive groups. At Oxford, for instance, there are not only college ties and club ties. There are also *staircase* ties.

A fairly new development in England is the occasion tie—and, for some reason, the occasion celebrated is usually unpleasant. So you have the pink elephant tie for hang-overs, the rain-stop-play tie for wet afternoons at Lord's, the dog-house tie for trouble with your wife. Whether anyone actually wears these ties I don't know. But they are manufactured, and people certainly buy them.

The club tie has gone round the collar-wearing world. Americans love them, and a notable recent feature of the

Madison Avenue men's shops has been the ousting of the smart 'continental' or Italian tie by scores and scores of different arrangements of dreary British club-type stripes. Chinese business men in Singapore dote on club ties. The late Mr Guy Burgess took his Old Etonian tie into Moscow exile with him; and that distinguished ex-rebel, Mr Jomo Kenyatta, replaces his worn-out London University ties whenever he comes to London; he is a man who doesn't like a shabby tie.

Still, these ties remain, all the same, a peculiarly English institution. Even though he may not wear it very often almost every Englishman has at least one tie that proclaims that he belongs to something. And at moments of doubt he can look at that tie, take it in his hands, put it round his neck. Then, truly, he knows he exists. He is someone. Furthermore, he is not alone. Somewhere there are others like him who can also wear this tie. There are times when he needs to know.

Opposite, upper row, from left to right: Royal Naval Volunteer Reserve; King's Own Scottish Borderers; Honourable Artillery Company; Royal Air Force Volunteer Reserve; Fleet Air Arm.

Opposite, lower row, from left to right: St Bartholomew's Hospital; The London Hospital; Guy's Hospital; Westminster Hospital; St Thomas's Hospital.

All the ties illustrated were provided by courtesy of Messrs C. H. Munday, Ltd., of Irving Street, Leicester Square.

Top row, left to right: Old Etonian; Harrow Association; Old Wykhamist; Old Pauline; Old Rugbeian.
Lower row, left to right: Old Marlburian; Old Haileyburian; Old Wellingtonian; Old Carthusian (Charterhouse); Old Citizens (City of London School).

'op row, left to right: Oxford University; Cambridge University; London 'niversity; Edinburgh University; Nottingham University.
ower row, left to right: Royal Navy; Royal Artillery; Royal Air Force; Royal Iarines; Brigade of Guards.

LAMENT
for the walking stick

MARGARET ALDRED

THE CARRYING of a stick, like that of a gun, can give a peculiar feeling of power to even the most gentle-minded person. It knows no barrier of age, for a boy with a stick cut from a hedge feels a man as he swaggers along whirling his stick. A woman has no doubt at all that she is safe from attack both inside and outside the house while carrying Great-Aunt Agatha's Alpine stick. The walker clad in tweeds, with a shaggy mountain of a dog at his heels, grasps his stick like a club and feels at one with primitive man. Maybe it is a throw-back to the shillelaghs, the sword sticks, and loaded canes.

The staff or walking stick has been a part of man since he first reared himself upon two legs. References in the Bible are numerous in allusions to a staff or rod. The rod of Moses proved more powerful than the sceptre of Pharaoh and the staff of Elisha restored the Shumanite child to life. Homer speaks of Grecian heroes as 'sceptre-bearing princes', and Agamemnon is said never to have gone forth without his staff of royalty, the sign of his authority.

Ancient Egyptian memorials and monuments show people of authority with tall slender staves crowned with lotus; but sticks having crooks and knobs have also been found in Egypt. An ancient carving shows one of the kings of Nineveh bearing a staff in his hand.

The staff was invaluable to pilgrims, an essential part of their equipment. On the road to the Holy Land, to Canterbury, to Walsingham, each pilgrim had his bourdon, a stick about five feet high, with a spiked foot to aid in climbing rough or steep places. About a foot from the top of the stick was a handle to give a firm grip and also to enable the pilgrim to remove fruit from bushes and trees. The bourdon was also a treasure-chest, for halfway down there was a joint which, when unscrewed, revealed a hollow into which the pilgrims placed their valuables, such as pilgrim medals of lead or glass, or a few coins, or—regrettable to record—contraband.

If it had not been for the bourdon the saffron trade would not have reached this country when it did, for according to Holinshed the first saffron flower was brought from Greece to England in one such bourdon at a time when it was death to take the plant out of Greece. In the same way a couple of silkworms were smuggled into southern Europe to enrich the clothes of women with their beautiful silk. On returning from a pilgrimage the wanderer tied a bunch of palm round the head of his bourdon, which has given us the word 'palmer'.

In *The Rape of the Lock* there is a reference to 'the nice conduct of a clouded cane', and this is enlarged upon in No. 103 of *The Tatler* (1709), where, following a plea for its continuance, the writer goes on to say that 'it had become as indispensable as any other of his limbs, and the knocking of it upon his shoe, leaning one leg upon it, or whistling upon it with his mouth, are such great relief to him in conversation that he does not know how he should be good company without it'.

By the late eighteenth century walking sticks both for men and women were as tall as the average man and not unlike the sticks carried by footmen on state occasions when they rode behind the coaches. Sticks have taken many strange forms, often quite at variance with the proud owner. A shrimp of a man would carry a stick like primitive man's club; a most honourable and mild man might walk proudly with a stick twisted like a serpent; the veriest landlubber parade with a stick made from the spine of a shark; the armchair traveller display a stick made of rhinoceros skin; the man who would rather die than face life on a farm use a stick made from the horns of a ram; and the potential murderer would carry a harmless little cane.

Those charming glass walking sticks filled with coloured sand, and today keenly sought by collectors, were of course not for use.

At the Great Exhibition of 1851 a collection of walking sticks was shown, including some with very curious uses. One stick concealed a miniature wine-cellar, and another a tiny larder, another a collection of maps. Another became a camp-stool, and, a characteristic Victorian practical joke, another stick gave an electric shock when gripped.

In the nineteenth century the trade in walking sticks was centred upon London, and orders came from every part of the world. One wholesale dealer boasted he had thousands of pounds in sticks. Each year this merchant prepared one and a half million rattans for umbrella ribs, and in one year he sold 509,000 manufactured walking sticks.

There was a limited trade in odd-shaped pieces of wood for sticks, and these fetched a good price. The carving of grotesque figures and heads on stick handles is probably traceable to the batons carried once by the fools or court jesters. A famous sculptor found his patron through his ability to carve patterns on a stick. Francis Chantrey was a milk-boy in the neighbourhood of Sheffield and in his spare time he would carve on sticks taken from the hedges; it was this idle carving which led to his becoming the possessor of an immense fortune, which he left for the encouragement of art—the Chantrey Bequest.

In Victorian London, according to *London Labour and the London Poor*, the selling of sticks was conducted mainly in the streets and almost entirely upon a Sunday. As many as one hundred stick dealers were sometimes in the streets on a Sunday, all making a living.

Today, in the cities and towns the only form in which the stick has survived is the rolled umbrella. Even in the country it is rare to see a walking stick. The military cane—not at all the same thing as a walking stick—still has a limited currency. But one never sees the dandy's cane, so reminiscent of the high dog-cart and the Edwardian boater, or the whippy cane beloved of Charlie Chaplin, and, as many a middle-aged man can ruefully testify, frequently used in the schools of yesterday for a purpose not intended by the manufacturer.

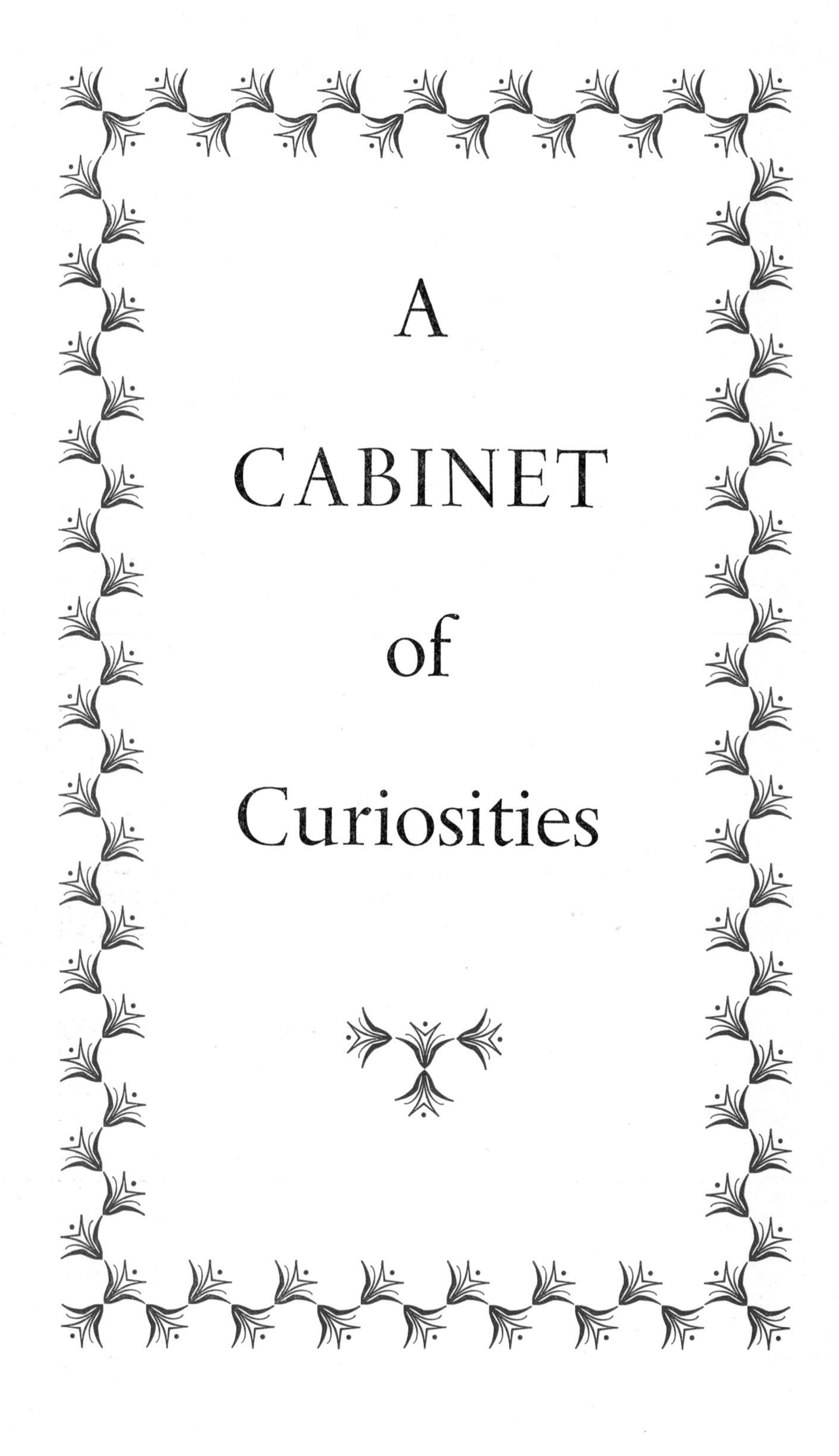

A CABINET of Curiosities

ARCIMBOLDO: The Librarian. *Skokloster, Sweden*

ARCIMBOLDO: Summer, from The Four Seasons. *Private Collection, London*

Arcimboldo

BERNARD DENVIR

THE ORDERED security of nature is not always as immutable as we hope. The potentialities of anarchy, which we keep carefully hidden from our conscious mind, find easier expression in the less inhibited idioms of the tongue. People become cabbages, violets, pansies, wallflowers, geese, donkeys, lambs; our footsteps are hampered by red herrings, our larders stocked with humble pies and sour grapes; our looks speak daggers, and even white Caucasians can be turned black by anger or green by envy. The world of speech is a world of the miraculous.

The intellect, of course, firmly repudiates this overthrow of reason, and brings it to heel by describing it as metaphor. But from what level of human experience are metaphors derived? Why do we need them? What shapes their form? Give in to a metaphor—allow it a breath of life, and you have a work of art, the formal expression of a truth too intricate for the simple clothing of language, too interwoven with the deeper strands of our existence for the comforting camouflage of logic.

Fantasy is as old as man. It springs from the same basic belief which has made him what he is—the illusion that eventually, in some way, at some time, or on some plane of existence, everything which exists can be brought under his control. It may be a pathetic fallacy, but it is an extremely emotive one; at its best it leads to the bravery of Pascal's 'if the whole universe were to overwhelm man, he would still be superior to it, for he would know what had overwhelmed him'; at its worst to the neurotic mumbo-jumbo of black magic. Above all else it is the motive force of man's creative life.

Faced with the intractability of matter, we create our private universe; we people it with our own creatures, adorn it with our own landscape, and subject it to rules of our own making. All those hybrid monsters which have peopled the myths and religions of the past—sphinxes, griffons, angels, satyrs, gargoyles, mermaids, Assyrian lion-men, and the whole pantheon of

Egypt's gods—are gestures of defiance against the implacable rigidity of a nature which will not admit to being our slave.

In our imagination we are lords and makers of universes, but the shapes which we create stem from a kind of historic human sub-consciousness, and supply us with an iconography of the human spirit. That is why all forms of fantastic art are almost invariably closest to those who lack either the desire or the ability to control the expression of experience—peasants, children, those to whom religion is not only a mode of life, but the sum total of existence, and the mentally disordered.

For centuries man's creative gestures against a scheme of things which owes nothing to his will, and repudiates his desires, were limited to the marrying of incompatible categories with one another. The choir stalls of medieval abbeys, the façades of Indian temples, the pages of Italian breviaries and the patterns of Oriental textiles proliferate with the fruits of imaginative miscegenation: boars with the heads of fishes, birds with the bodies of dogs, men with the talons of eagles.

It was not till the sixteenth century that there appeared anyone with the imaginative vigour and technical skill to express one form of life in terms of another; to use the forms of nature for creating a compound, not a mixture. We can still feel the impact of his discovery across the centuries.

His name was Giuseppe Arcimboldo, and it is significant that not only was he born under the shadow of that great lexicon of fantastic imagery, the Duomo of Milan, but that his father Biagio was one of the masons concerned with the upkeep of its fabric. His mind was formed and his imagination nurtured in a world of mystery which, medieval in form, derived its content from a tradition which was ancient when Christ was born. His life began under the shadow of the great cathedral, and when he died in 1593 at the age of sixty-six he was buried in it. His first known work was a statue of the Virgin, which he carved for the façade, and the record of the payment which he received for it still exists. There are also grounds for believing that he may have helped his father in the design of a window depicting the martyrdom of St Catherine.

In an earlier age, in a different civilization, his life would have continued along these lines. He would have joined the multitude of anonymous craftsmen to whom we owe most of the great symbols of Western civilization. But this was the sixteenth century, and when we hear of his moving from Milan to the court of Hercule d'Este, at Ferrara, we recognize a symptom of the times.

The world of the Renaissance became to the men who lived in it daily more improbable. Its new realities were more incredible than the mysteries of an earlier generation. Columbus had discovered America, not invented it; the routine efficiency of the solar system turned out to be more impressive than the old unheard music of the crystal spheres. As ancient landmarks of belief vanished, there was a frenzied search for new ones to take their place.

Science—the phrase Natural Philosphy which often describes it in the older seats of learning is suggestive—was an imaginative rather than an empirical exercise, and it had not yet hardened down into a body of dogma. Men who made discoveries which profoundly influence our lives even today, made them in laboratories cluttered up with unicorns' horns, witches' toenails, fragments from Noah's ark, and the dried blood of basilisks. And often enough they were trying to discover, not the truths with which we now accredit them, but the secret of perpetual motion, or how to turn everything into gold.

It seemed as though the only limits which could be set on knowledge were the potentialities of the human imagination; and the inevitable corollary of this was that artists were called upon to perform the tasks which today would be undertaken by scientists, technologists, engineers. The universality of Leonardo's interests was not unique. We are impressed by it mainly because he was a genius of outstanding ability, and because his notebooks have survived to bear witness to its processes.

When Arcimboldo went to the court of Ferrara he was moving not only from one city to another, but from the Middle Ages to the Renaissance. The d'Estes had always been remarkable for their patronage of the arts, for their lively curiosity, and for their ability to attract to their service the most diverse talents. Hercule was no exception, and he, more than anyone else, must have been responsible for transforming the young cathedral craftsman into an explorer of that other new world which man was discovering within himself.

It was at Ferrara too that Arcimboldo first came into contact with the Flemmings, working at the Duke's tapestry works, who were disseminating in Italy that taste for what a later generation would call the 'surreal'; for that marriage of dream and reality, expressed in a technique whose meticulous accuracy makes it all the more frightening, which found its highest expression in the works of Hieronymus Bosch and Pieter Brueghel.

Ferrara was no more than a stopping place. By 1560 Arcimboldo had found his spiritual home, the environment which was to nourish his strange gifts, stimulate his imagination, and enable him to contribute so vividly to the history of human experience. He was summoned to the court of the Hapsburgs, which, moving in ritual solemnity from Vienna to Prague at fixed seasons of the year, was like the living embodiment of some scenario conceived by a megalomaniac film director of the Weimar Republic vintage. It combined the worlds of Faust and Dr Caligari.

As court painter, first to Maximilian II and then to Rudolph II, Arcimboldo lived in a world where improbability was the stuff of everyday life. Both emperors were collectors on a gargantuan scale, imperial magpies to whom wealth and power made everything accessible, and on whose passion for possession the whole museum structure of twentieth-century Europe is built. Their lust for acquisition was equalled only by their lack of discrimination.

Side by side with masterpieces which are still the crowning possessions of the Vienna Kunsthistorisches Museum, they amassed samples of the Virgin's milk, segments of Jason's fleece, mandragora roots which gave forth human cries when they were cut, the profile of Satan frozen, at some unguarded moment, into the structure of a rock crystal. Rudolph especially, a morose, neurotic man, who would spend weeks shut up in his cabinet of curiosities, and whose chair, on which, they say, he used to sit to conjure up the Devil, is still one of the attractions of Prague, was especially fascinated by the abnormal. It would seem almost as though he found consolation for his own lack of stability in the existence of anything which hinted at a more cosmic disorder. Two-headed babies, bearded women, hermaphrodites, dwarfs, giants, and other freaks were brought to him at any cost, from any quarter of the globe. And when the realities could not be acquired he had pictures painted of them, devoting a whole section of his enormous art gallery to the portraiture of horrors.

It is probable that Arcimboldo must already have started at Ferrara to paint those fantastic portraits composed of natural objects which are always associated with his name, and that it was these which were responsible for his being summoned to the court of the Holy Roman Emperor. For more than twenty years he continued to produce these strange reconstructions of the human image, spurred on by his delighted patrons to ever greater efforts.

All the great officers of the court were transformed by him at the Emperor's command into mixtures of plants, vegetables, and the like. Rudolph himself became 'Autumn'; and, when the higher echelons had been exhausted, gardeners, the court doctor, whose nose was already transformed by the ravages of what was currently described as the 'morbus Gallicus' far more effectively than ever it could have been by the imagination of an artist, and the royal librarian were also subjected to the same metamorphosis.

The popularity of these paintings was immediate and complete. Poets such as Comanini wrote laudatory verses about them; imitators sprang up all over Europe. Arcimboldo himself was created a Count by a grateful master, and even, according to his friend Morigia, who was currently engaged on writing a history of Milan, entrusted with delicate diplomatic missions.

The age, of course, was especially sensitive to the common links between man and the universe. Matter had an infinite variability,

> Of his bones are coral made,
> These are pearls that were his eyes,
> Nothing of him that doth fade,
> But doth suffer a sea change,
> Into something rich and strange.

There had already been hints and foreshadowings of the same preoccupation. The ancients had robed Dionysus in a dress made of plants; Bacchic masks were composed of vine leaves, and Indian artifacts—quite a number had found their way into the Hapsburg collections—paid tribute in their amalgam of living phenomena to the belief that all life possessed in time and place a sacred unity. But Arcimboldo had evolved a new, personal, and highly successful formula of complete integration.

Stylistically he was a craftsman. His vivid, meticulous realism, which must have been based on a detailed study of the natural phenomena which he used for his visual vocabulary, equals, when it does not surpass, that of the Dutch flower-painters of the following century. He has an exquisite sense of colour. 'Water' might well be a Whistlerian tone-poem in grey with its occasional notes of red and blue. Yet the bright notations against the sombre background are not fortuitous. Always they help to create the expression of the face, hinting at unexpected suggestions of irony, disdain, or self-satisfaction. His ingenuity, though not of itself a creative attribute, is manifest. To create 'Water' he used no less than a hundred and seventy-three different forms of marine fauna, deploying them with a mesmeric skill, and though 'The Librarian' is a *tour de force* of manipulation, it is not irrelevant to remember that in creating a body from cubes, rectangles, and the primary forms of geometry, Arcimboldo was anticipating the doctrines of Cézanne and painting the first Cubist picture.

It would be doing an injustice to him, and a disservice to our own potentialities of enjoyment, were we to deny his great technical gifts. But they do not explain his immediate success, nor do they account for his long stream of imitators—sophisticated Mannerist painters, hack producers of political caricatures, greetings-card manufacturers, the designers of those crude prints which depict artisans, constructed from the tools of their trade, which adorned the walls of so many nineteenth-century homes. More recently the appearance of the *Vegetabull* on the hoardings of Britain suggested that the Arcimboldo formula has not lost its potency.

It is the images which fascinate; the creation of human faces out of non-human materials, elaborate visual metaphors which repel and intrigue, hypnotize and alarm by their strange perversion of the natural order of things.

Man tends to measure his aesthetic pleasures by the varying degrees to which they cater for two antithetical desires; one for security and reassurance, the other for heightened experience, for the exhilaration of danger, for anything which sharpens the awareness of existence. He finds satisfaction in the controlled, formalized struggle of chess, and in the lonely dangers of mountaineering. In the language of art the same contrast is expressed in the classical and the romantic; in an ordering of the world of external phenomena, in which nothing is left to chance, everything is secure and inevitable, in which content is matched by style, the image by the forms which express it; or alternatively, in a visual or auditory assault on the imagination, a rejection of all sense of logic and security, an exposure of the nerves of the imagination to those sensations which, by their threat of the unexpected, dissolve our sense of certainty and awaken an apprehensive thrill of pure sensation.

Arcimboldo's works are outstanding examples of this second category, of a tradition which has included works as disparate as Grünewald's 'Crucifixion', the guillotined heads painted by Géricault, Gaudi's cathedral of Barcelona, and the works of doctrinaire surrealists such as Dali and Max Ernst. There is something essentially ambiguous in the vision of a face constructed from flowers, of a chin which forms part of a landscape, of an ear made out of a mushroom. We cannot, as the saying goes, believe our senses, because in some curious way we do not want to, and in savouring this overthrow of nature, we vindicate that philosophy of existence which Sartre expressed in the saying that consciousness is that which it is not, and is not that which it is.

The vitality of these paintings may be due in part to the fact that they are pure fantasy. The age was one of symbolism, and countless other artists, as well as writers, evolved the most complex and elaborate vocabulary of symbolic form. But apart from the obvious relationship between the titles which he gave his paintings, and the elements from which he composed them,

Arcimboldo made no attempt at creating any kind of internal logic, no matter how imaginative. Fantasy alone guided him.

It had been as Hofmaler, or portrait painter, that Arcimboldo first made his appearance on the registers of the Imperial Household, and, in addition to the heads, we know that he painted a composite portrait of all members of the Hapsburg family—living and dead—in itself a hint at the strange quality of his imagination. Inevitably too he was pressed into the creation of those elaborate theatrical fantasies which helped to shelter the courtiers of Prague and Vienna from the alarming realities of the world in which they lived. One book of designs for such schemes is preserved in the Uffizi at Florence, and in Boston there are thirteen drawings by him composed for Baron Hoffman of Grunbuchel, President of the Imperial Council at Prague. Included in these is his only known autograph in the form of a letter to the Baron in which he defends the imagery of the grotesque, pointing out that it had been practised by the ancients, and apologizes for the fact that owing to the pressure of commissions for the Emperor he had not had time to complete the Baron's work.

One other fascinating fact we know about Arcimboldo is that he invented a method of colometric transcription of music which anticipated the actual procedure for film and sound synchronization used in the twentieth century, expressing notes by visual forms and colours which were 'read' by Monzo, a viola player of Cremona.

It is virtually impossible now to catalogue all the works which Arcimboldo produced during his stay at the Imperial Court. The 'Four Seasons' exist in several versions, one in Vienna, another, reproduced here, was given by Elizabeth, the Winter Queen, wife of the Elector Palatine Frederick V, and sister of Charles I, to Lord Craven, a busy Stuart diplomat who had interested himself in her affairs. Both these sets are signed, the Viennese version in the 'Spring' painting, the English one on the collar of 'Summer'. There were probably several other versions of the same theme, as individual items exist in other collections. Comparable to this series was one of 'The Elements', to which 'Fire' and 'Water' belong. This also existed in several

ARCIMBOLDO: Fire. *Kunsthistorisches Museum, Vienna*

ARCIMBOLDO: Winter, from The Four Seasons. *Private Collection, London*

ARCIMBOLDO: Autumn, from The Four Seasons. *Private Collection, London*

ARCIMBOLDO: Water. *Kunsthistorisches Museum, Vienna*

versions, two of which are known to us at second hand from drawings of them by Heinrich Goding, a seventeenth-century Saxon artist, which, strangely enough, belonged at one time to Theo Van Gogh, Vincent's art-dealing brother. One group of Arcimboldo's works found their way into Sweden as a result of the sack of Prague during the Thirty Years War, amongst them 'The Librarian'.

Having obtained permission to retire from his court position in 1587, Arcimboldo returned to Milan, and died there six years later. Even before then imitators had started copying his style—for this was an age which had no keen sense of copyright, and which attached to the question of authenticity little of the economic significance which it possesses today. The imitators varied greatly in technical skill and imaginative ability, and they have gravely complicated the problem of which paintings out of several score, apart from those which are completely documented, can be attributed to the master himself. But they form a coherent school which still exerts an influence in such unlikely quarters as advertising posters, political caricatures, and typographical design. As an empirical fantasist Arcimboldo is one of the supreme masters of what Odilon Redon described as 'that sense of mystery which is always to be found in the equivocal, in double and treble aspects, in hints of aspects and in the existence of an image within an image'.

Citizen Train

MIRIAM ALLEN DE FORD

ON EVERY sunny day during the 1890s a lean old gentleman with a mop of white hair used to sit in Madison Square, New York, surrounded—indeed, overrun—by children. They climbed all over him, sat in his lap, gathered around him and listened as he talked by the hour. He was provided with a bag of peanuts, which he shared impartially between the children and the pigeons—not forgetting himself, for he lived for the most part on peanuts and water.

Citizen George Francis Train was holding his daily court.

Should an adult approach and speak to him, Citizen Train would not answer. He kept a pad and pencil by him, and wrote his reply to any question; or, if that involved too much labour, he said in a loud voice to the nearest child: 'Tell him'—whatever he wished to communicate. Should the adult extend his hand in greeting, Citizen Train ignored the gesture but solemnly shook hands with himself. He was storing up psychic force, and did not intend to dissipate it by speaking to or touching any grown human being.

He lived for $3 a week in Mills Hotel No. 1, on Bleecker Street. Ogden Mills, who had founded these hotels for the poor, was one of his closest friends. The walls of Train's room were completely covered with pictures, letters, and cuttings, some of which were evidence—if evidence were needed—that once he had had two large houses of his own, and spent $2,000 a week. His married daughter in Stamford, Connecticut, whose husband was an official of the New York Subtreasury, always kept a room for him, but he preferred his independence, the pigeons, and the children. He was far from bankrupt. He still owned 5,000 lots in Omaha, Nebraska, for which he had paid $175 apiece, and which were currently valued at $40,000,000. But they were held in trust for him, since he had been declared legally insane.

Few men were ever saner.

Despite his peculiarities, the old gentleman was far from

senile. Two years before he died at seventy-four, he had dictated his autobiography in thirty-five hours, and it is a persuasive and coherent work. Of course, he had a high opinion of himself. He told Will Carleton that he was 'the greatest man in the world'. But that didn't mean he was crazy. Look at what he had done.

He was a shipping magnate before he was of age, owner of the famous *Flying Cloud* built by David McKay of East Boston, which had beaten all the Baltimore clippers by sailing from New York to San Francisco in sixty-eight days. He was one of the founders of the Union Pacific Railroad. He had picked out the site of Tacoma, Washington, as the terminus of the Northern Pacific Railroad. He had established the first trust, the Crédit Mobilier —and was out of it long before the scandal concerning its financing arose. He had introduced the first street railways into England, Switzerland, and Denmark. In his early twenties he had been a prominent business man in Liverpool and in Melbourne. He had anticipated Jules Verne by going around the world in eighty days in 1870. In 1868 he was offered the Democratic vice-presidential candidacy with Salmon P. Chase for president (he declined unless Chase was willing to reverse the offices); and in 1872 he nominated himself for president on an independent ticket, charged admission to his campaign meetings, and ended up with few votes but with $90,000 profit!

He was acquainted with Napoleon III and the Empress Eugénie, and persuaded Queen Maria Cristina of Spain to put all her funds (disastrously) into his Atlantic and Great Western Railroad (now a part of the Erie System). Nevertheless, he was also aide to Gustave Paul Cluseret, military chief of the Paris Commune, and saved Cluseret's life from Gambetta's soldiers by wrapping himself in the French and American flags and daring the men to fire—while Cluseret made his escape. He was thick in the councils of the Irish Fenians, and was offered the presidency of a republic of Australian miners which never came off. He was gaoled sixteen times 'without ever having committed a crime'.

He was the first person to suggest—to inventors who patented and profited by his ideas—erasers attached to pencils, perforations between postage stamps, steps attached to carriages, packaging tea in paper bags, ink bottles with a nose to prevent spilling, and chutes in coal-carts to let the coal out instead of having it unloaded in sacks. He was the father of the salmon-packing industry in Oregon. He was the first person to expose the notorious Tweed Ring in New York.

He also walked naked on the street on one occasion, amused himself by filling in a prison register blank in Boston with 'Color: Octoroon', never wore a hat (in the days when that was unheard of), and deluged New York and Brooklyn newspapers with post-card messages on current topics, written endwise, crosswise, and every other way with a double-headed red and blue pencil. A lifelong Free Thinker, he gave Sunday-evening lectures on texts parodied from the Bible—for example: 'Hit 'is eye, be not afraid.'

And still he was not insane: he was merely completely and entirely himself. As he himself put it:

> Many persons attribute to me simply an impulsiveness and an impressibility, as if I were some erratic comet, rushing madly through space, emitting coruscations of fancifully colored sparks, without system, rule, or definite object. This is a popular error. I claim to be a close analytical observer of passing events, applying the crucible of Truth to every new matter or subject presented to my mind or my senses.

George Francis Train was born in Boston on March 24, 1829. His father, Oliver Train, had married Maria Pickering, eldest daughter of George Pickering, a slave-owner from Baltimore who had been converted to Methodism, freed his slaves, and become an itinerant Methodist preacher at a salary of $200 a year. He was able to survive under these circumstances because he had married the heiress of a thousand-acre farm near Waltham, Massachusetts, which was his home thereafter. The Pickerings claimed descent from Judge Gilbert Pickering, one of the court which had condemned Charles I to execution. Another of their ancestors was Timothy Pickering, a member of Washington's first cabinet.

The Pickering daughters as they married brought their husbands to live on the farm, and formed one large patriarchal family. But before 1830, when George Francis was still an infant, Oliver Train took his family (there were three older sisters) to New Orleans, where he opened a grocery store. George Francis claimed to remember everything in his life from the age of three, and certainly had an exact memory of New Orleans.

In 1833 yellow fever struck the town. Train has left a vivid picture, reminiscent of Defoe's *Journal of the Plague Year*, of the epidemic—the 'dead cart' coming around at night, with the driver calling 'Bring out your dead!', and then the hastily constructed coffins being tossed on top of those already there. One by one, the three little girls succumbed. The mother was next. Then the maternal grandmother, back in Waltham, wrote to Oliver Train to send his remaining child to her before he too fell a victim.

So at the age of four little George Francis was put aboard ship for Boston, wearing a badge which read: 'This is my little son George Francis Train, four years old, consigned on board the ship *Henry* . . . to be sent to his grandmother Pickering in Waltham, ten miles from Boston. Take good care of the little fellow as he is the only one left of eleven of us in the house, including the servants. I will come as soon as I can arrange my business.'

The last George Francis Train saw of his father was a lonely figure waving to him from the wharf, trying to conceal his grief lest he move the child to tears. Nothing more was ever heard of him. He too undoubtedly died of yellow fever.

The voyage lasted twenty-three days. The rough sailors were kind to 'the little fellow', though they taught him to swear so fluently that he horrified his grandparents when he arrived. The sailors certainly did not bother to wash him; he had not seen soap or water or changed his clothes for more than three weeks when his uncle collected him in Boston. Nevertheless—or in consequence—he had a glorious time. By way of amusing themselves, the men used to climb up in the rigging and throw lumps of sugar down to the boy. They told him that up there in the rigging, too far for him to see, there was a marvellous plantation, and that it was the monkeys in this plantation who threw the sugar at him. He believed them implicitly, and at once told the story to his grandmother and aunts. When they laughed at him he was outraged, and when they tried to clean him up he refused absolutely to let them touch him until they told him they credited his story. (Train used to say that he had never told a lie in his life.) The four-year-old pitted his will against that of his elders, and won. It took three days of struggle, but finally his grandmother gave in and agreed that the plantation existed, and George Francis allowed her to give him a bath. It was his first conquest.

Incidentally, the voyage made a Free Thinker of him. On reflection, he finally realized that the sailors had been spoofing him. He applied the same criterion to everything he was told which could not be proved, from Santa Claus to God, and decided then and there that he was through with all of them. He won his second battle when he refused to kneel for daily prayers in that Methodist household; and again, against his implacable obstinacy, the grown-ups backed down.

Rather remarkably, in view of this episode, his grandmother wanted to make a minister of the bright little orphan. That hope naturally died a-borning, though it gave him three months of study with a clergyman in Framingham when he was fourteen—to which he used to refer afterwards as 'my college education'. Until that time the only schooling he received was three months every summer in a one-room school. George Francis was regularly and monotonously at the head of the school; he was a precocious child, who read every one of the dozen books in the farmhouse over and over, and filled out his reading with the only newspaper taken in by the Pickerings, the Methodist *Zion's Herald.*

From the beginning, as far as his strength allowed, he helped with the chores of the farm, as the smallest children were expected to do in those days, and from the time he was ten he took the produce every week to the Boston market, sold it, bought needed supplies, and drove home again. He was justified in saying he had supported himself from his babyhood.

After his three months with the clergyman he made it finally clear that he was *not* going to follow his grandfather into the Church, and set out for Boston to find a job. Very soon he became errand boy and boy-of-all-work for a druggist, at $2 a month. One day the druggist went out and left him in charge. He sampled 'every candy and syrup' in stock, then, his appetite only whetted, bought himself raw oysters and lemonade. The result may be imagined. For some reason, instead of blaming his own gluttony, he felt the drug business was responsible, and quit it cold. He walked to Cambridgeport and found himself another eighteen-hour-a-day job with a grocer there. Here he stayed for three years.

One afternoon a man walked into the grocery who was a first cousin of his father's, Colonel Enoch Train, head of a big shipping company. The Colonel was astonished to discover the boy's identity; he had been Oliver Train's closest friend as well as his cousin, and had supposed that the entire family had been wiped out in the yellow-fever epidemic in New Orleans. George Francis was fascinated by his employer's account of the Colonel's wealth and importance and the scope of his business. The next day he turned up at Enoch Train's office and demanded a position.

The Colonel might as well have given up without a struggle. No argument made any impression: there was no opening, the boy was too young, he knew nothing of the business. None of that mattered. There he was, and he calmly seated himself at a desk and asked what he should do to start. Feebly the Colonel made a last effort—he handed George Francis a large number of bills to be transposed from English to American currency, thinking that his inability to handle the work would be a final excuse for getting rid of him. Blithely Train asked the rate of exchange, set to work, and finished in record time. The Colonel knew when he was beaten. George Francis was an employee from then on.

Before he was twenty he was a partner, and was doing most of the executive work of the firm. At twenty-one he was sent to Liverpool to take care of the branch there. Before he went he asked for a vacation in which he could see his own country before living abroad for an indefinite period, and for two months he travelled from Washington to Niagara Falls—collecting autographs as he went, from Henry Clay, from Daniel Webster, from Zachary Taylor—autographs which he used later in Europe as credentials to enable him to meet any notables he ran across!

In a railway station in Syracuse he saw a beautiful girl with golden curls, and with an elderly escort. She was, they said, a Miss Davis (Train never did mention her given name), of Louisville, the daughter of Colonel Davis, aide-de-camp to General Winfield Scott in the Mexican War, and just seventeen.

'I'm going to marry her,' George Francis announced. So of course he did. He managed to get a seat across the aisle in the train, to enter into conversation, and to introduce himself. At Niagara Falls, while he showed off by risky cavortings under the spray of the Horseshoe Falls, they became engaged. He came back from England in 1851 to marry her, and they lived in the utmost happiness until she died in 1877. Their first daughter died in infancy, but they reared another, and two sons. There never was a rift in the family solidarity, however *outré* some of the things that happened to the husband and father.

In 1852 Train returned from Liverpool again, and proposed to Enoch Train that he receive a larger share of the profits of the firm, in view of his vital contributions to them. The old man lost his temper and accused George Francis of trying to freeze him out. George Francis kept his, won his point, and then tore up the new contract. 'If you think that of me,' he said, 'I don't want to have anything to do with you at all.' He set sail for Australia and opened a shipping and commission house of his own in Melbourne, which was soon making $95,000 a year.

In 1855 he made, with his family, the first of his round-the-world trips (with no attempt to break records this time), writing a book later on his experiences, as he had previously written one on his English adventures. In all he fathered a dozen books, all long ago out of print, and acted as occasional correspondent for both the *New York Herald* and the London *Times*. Most of his newspaper stories he signed 'Young America', the name sneeringly given to him by business rivals annoyed by his precocity and brashness. If he seemed to flit from one enterprise—or one industry—to another, it was always with an eye on the main chance.

He was in England when the Civil War started, and the series of lectures he gave pleading the Union cause undoubtedly helped to keep the British Government from declaring for the Confederacy. In his own country, however, he was accused of being a Copperhead, because (like Lincoln) he had no love for the Abolitionists, but wanted the Union preserved, with or without slavery.

Back in America after the war, while California's 'Big Four' (Crocker, Stanford, Huntingdon, and Hopkins) were pushing the Union Pacific from the west, Train was the chief organizer from the east. It was in this period, through his interest in importing Irish immigrants to work on the railroad and his concern with their welfare after they got there, that he first became more or less involved with the Fenians. (Once a telegram sent to a point in Canada, 'Train arriving on hunt', resulted in his being met by a military detachment bent on putting down a Fenian mob—till it was explained that George Francis Train was simply arriving on business on the ship *Hunt*!) He also spent some time in a Dublin gaol on charges of Fenianism.

But his career as a 'liberator' had really begun in 1852 when the Australian miners, aware of his constant sympathy with the underdog, named him as president of their abortive 'Five Star Republic'. In fact, except for the 'Ligue du Midi' episode in Marseilles with Cluseret during the Commune, Train was always a 'liberator' against his will. When he was hailed by Italian revolutionists in Rome he was seriously annoyed, since he had come there to conduct business with the Austrian overlords! He believed (and perhaps he was right) that spies had followed him ever since the Australian affair.

It is true that his heart beat warmly for the oppressed everywhere, that he had the almost fanatical love of independence of the old-time Yankee, and the missionary urge to spread its benefits over all the world. But it is equally true that he was never officially involved (even in France) in any revolutionary uprising, and that he had not the remotest idea, either in France or anywhere else, of the theories or principles behind these uprisings. His primary object in implicating himself in French politics in 1870 (with the consequence of spending two weeks in gaol in Lyons until Gambetta freed him—and expelled him from the country) was a desire to organize the beaten French to renew the war with Prussia!

All in all, the Citizen was six times legally declared insane—though he never was. The first time was in consequence of litigation arising from the financing of the Union Pacific. But the last and most celebrated time was in 1872, and the actuating cause was the famous Victoria Woodhull and her sister, Tennessee Claflin. (These ladies were not eccentrics; they were distinctly adventuresses, and very successful ones.) At this period Train was publishing a paper he called the *Train Ligue*—a title reminiscent of the 'Ligue du Midi' of Marseilles, during the Commune. When the sisters published, in their *Woodhull and Claflin's Weekly*, the first overt account of the notorious Beecher-Tilden adultery charges, they were promptly arrested for uttering an obscenity. Train flew to their defence, saying rightly that what they had written might be libellous, but was not obscene; and in his own magazine he published a long quotation from the Bible, ten times as obscene as anything printed in the *Weekly*.

He was accordingly in turn charged with the same offence, and lodged for some reason in 'Murderers' Row' in the Tombs. There were thirteen inmates in all, and they immediately formed a club and elected Train their president.

When his case came up for trial before Judge Noah Davis the judged charged the jury to declare Train insane. He promptly rose to his feet and moved the impeachment of the judge. But the jury did as it was told, and no matter how hard Train struggled to get himself tried on the charge for which he had been indicted, he never succeeded. He had already fought to stay in the Tombs until the matter was settled, but he was finally bailed out against his will. His family seems to have taken a hand, the object avowedly being to keep him from wasting his fortune.

If that was their aim it succeeded. From that time onward Train became completely uninterested in money after a lifetime spent in acquiring it. He moved to the attic of the Continental Hotel, at 19th Street and Broadway, and after Mills Hotel No. 1 was opened he moved there, stayed there for the rest of his life, and finally died there.

The obscenity arrest occurred at the very end of his independent campaign for president of the United States. The Citizen had had this project in mind ever since 1868, when Salmon P. Chase refused to change places with him and run for vice-president with Train for president. He honestly expected to be elected; he told Carleton that he was 'talking to the next president'. The reason for this expectation was not lunacy; it was a naive belief in the will of the American voters to elect as their president a man of brains and integrity who had their best interests at heart. He ran against Grant (up for his second term) and Horace Greeley. Greeley carried six states and died soon after, almost literally of a broken heart. Train carried no states at all, but his heart was far from broken. He was merely disgusted with the lack of acumen of his fellow citizens—and, after all, he was $90,000 to the good. Besides, by that time he was very busy trying to have himself tried as an utterer of obscenity instead of being brushed off as a madman.

He was not yet through with his prison experiences. One came in Boston in the 1890s, and grew directly out of the 1872 case. An obscure printer had come to Train's defence by copying in his own little paper part of Train's biblical quotation. Of course he was immediately arrested, convicted, and sentenced, and lost his business and his printing-press. Train helped him buy a new press on his release, and sixteen years later, as soon as he came within the jurisdiction of the seller of the still incompletely paid-for press, the latter had him arrested for the other man's debt.

It was on this occasion that Train filled out the registration blank as follows:

> Name: George Francis Train, more commonly known as 'Champion Crank'. Residence: Generally in jail! Color: Octoroon! Temperate? Yes (never tasted liquor). [He didn't smoke, either.] Property: own half Omaha when I choose to become sane. Occupation: Aristocratic loafer! Offence charged: Helping poor printer buy printing-press. Number of Times Committed: Twice for this one offense! In 14 [later 16] jails for telling truth! Sentence or Otherwise: So long as blackmailer pays my board. Non-Payment of Fines and Costs: Have not paid cash for anything, and don't intend to!

The plaintiff finally grew tired of paying Train's board and he was released.

His last brush with the law was in Stamford, less than a year before his death. While visiting his daughter, he contracted smallpox. It was a light case and he soon recovered, but meanwhile he had been taken to the pesthouse and his clothing had been destroyed. He threatened to sue the city for $50,000 for burning his clothes and manuscripts, and raised such a hullabaloo that the city fathers were glad to get rid of him by paying him $2,000.

Probably what irked him most was the fact that his hospitalization involved having to touch other people, for these were the years in which for the most part he communicated only with or through children. As late as 1893, however, he appeared for the last time in what might be called a public capacity. Hearing that the Chicago World's Fair was starting off badly and was likely to be a failure, he travelled to Chicago to 'save' it. And he did. He collected a Dahomey belle from the African Village on the Midway, organized a grand march through the grounds, and led it with the savage lady on his arm. Then he toured the Midwest on behalf of the Fair and saw it firmly on the way to success before he returned to New York.

In 1902, when he dictated his autobiography, *My Life in Many States and in Foreign Lands*, the Citizen announced that 'through psychic telepathy' he was 'doubling his age'. That should have meant that he expected to live nearly 150 years. If that was his expectation it is to be hoped that he did not realize he was dying, when less than two years later he succumbed to a heart attack in his little room in the 'Mills Palace'.

After his death Dr Edward C. Spitzka weighed Train's brain. It came to 1,525 grams (54 ounces)—the fifth heaviest known to science. That would have pleased him—except that he would have wanted first place instead of fifth.

Back in his youth a phrenologist had told George Francis Train that he would be 'either a great reformer or a great pirate'. He fulfilled the prediction twofold. He was both.

Breakfast with Oscar

BEVERLEY NICHOLS

ONE MIGHT have thought that the last story about him had been told, that the last *conte scandaleuse* had been dragged from the remotest volume of memoirs, and that the brains of every ancient Parisian *concierge* had been picked in the hope that in his guttersnipe days he might have been offered a glass of absinthe by the notorious Sebastian Melmoth.

But there is one story that has never been told, and I shall tell it here. And though it could be narrated in a very few words, that is not how I propose to go about it. For this story is vintage Oscar. Besides, it needs an introduction.

ILLUM CRIMEN HORRIBILE QUOD NON NOMINANDUM EST

The scene was the bedroom of a rambling Victorian house in Torquay. I was rising fifteen and I had been rudely awakened from an innocent sleep, in the small hours of the morning, by a burly man with a thick black moustache. My father. He strode over to the window and tore back the curtain with a simple gesture. Then he sat down at my desk and began to write.

I rubbed my eyes and blinked at him with some astonishment. He was evidently in a towering rage. After a few moments he threw down his pencil, rose to his feet, and glared at me as though I were something unclean.

He pointed to the desk with a trembling finger. 'That,' he shouted, 'is what That Man did.' With which he stalked from the room, slamming the door behind him. I was still scarcely awake, but I slid out of bed, and took up the paper on which he had written, in block capitals, this macabre message: ILLUM CRIMEN HORRIBILE . . . 'that horrible crime which is not to be named'.

Then it all came back in a flood of humiliating memory . . . the violent scene of the night before, my mother's tears, and the flames creeping round my beautiful book, the book bound in white parchment powdered with silver fleurs-de-lis, the book which Reggie had given me. *The Picture of Dorian Gray.*

Reggie was a neighbour of ours, in his early thirties. He was rich, volatile, and extremely popular with the old ladies who formed the majority of Torquay's population. Nowadays it would have been screamingly obvious to everybody that he was a homosexual. His walk, his clothes, the sinuous gestures of his delicately manicured hands—he was a parody of the low comedian's conventional portrait of a 'sissy'. But Torquay was still sunk deep in the dark ages as far as *that* sort of thing was concerned. Never for a moment did it occur to anybody that his mannerisms might be more than amiable eccentricities. 'Dear Reggie is so artistic,' murmured the dowagers as they sipped their tea in his elegant drawing-room, which was lavishly decorated with photographs of his equally artistic young friends in Taormina—sun-burned fisher-boys who appeared to spend the greater part of their lives in the nude. Even when he came to lunch with his cheeks heavily rouged my mother was merely amused. 'Dear Reggie has actually begun to "touch up",' she observed. 'I wonder whatever he will do next?'

What he did next was to give me *The Picture of Dorian Gray*.

I was a very good-looking boy, but I was also a strangely innocent one. On the evenings when I went to dine with him, which always ended with music, I sometimes wished that he would not breathe so heavily down the back of my neck when I was playing Chopin, but I suspected nothing sinister. The only thing which disturbed me, ever so faintly, was his apparent anxiety to make me drunk. At the age of fifteen a little Médoc and a glass of vintage port are enough to produce a considerable exhilaration, but at these dinners, when we were served by a young Greek footman who might have posed for Praxiteles, there was always champagne, and Armagnac, and an assortment of liqueurs as colourful as the celebrated passage about the jewels in *Dorian Gray* . . . green Chartreuse and yellow Chartreuse, Benedictine and Curaçao, Kümmel and Crème de Menthe and Cointreau . . . especially Cointreau. I excused myself on the grounds that Cointreau was bad for the cadenzas.

The present of *Dorian Gray*, which arrived on the morning of my fifteenth birthday, was presumably intended to produce another form of intoxication, and in this it certainly succeeded.

As I have already mentioned, it was bound in white parchment powdered with silver fleurs-de-lis, but even if it had been a paperback I should have fallen under its heady spell. From the moment when the curtain rose on the studio scene, with the scent of lilacs drifting through the open window, I was enthralled. True, some of the epigrams were a little over my head, and sometimes I felt faintly cheated because the author was so very mysterious about what Dorian actually *did* that was so unspeakably wicked. (In my innocence I suspected that it must be something to do with naked women.) But these were minor drawbacks to the sheer enchantment of page after page of purple prose, as heavily encrusted with jewels as a Fabergé cigarette-case. This, I thought, was one of the great masterpieces of all time. Odd as it may seem, I still think so.

All through that long golden day of April I pored over *Dorian Gray*, and in the evening my father found me reading it in the garden by the light of the dying sun. His reaction, as we have seen, was swift and brutal. When he hurled the book into the fire he shouted that he was sending it back to its accursed author, who was burning in the quenchless fires of hell. And when I dared to ask: 'Why? What did he *do*?' he could find no words to answer me in the English language. It was a curious introduction to the problems of homosexuality.

What has this to do with our story? Little, except to date it—and to stress the shock it made upon me when at last it came.

First the date. That was thirty years later. Incredibly, during those three long decades, the name of Oscar Wilde was never mentioned in our household. Europe might burst into flames—and did—Evil incarnate might stalk abroad—and did—but the author of *The Importance of Being Earnest* represented a sort of Evil beyond Evil. He was the ultimate horror . . . the Thing.

And then, quite suddenly and casually, my mother mentioned that he had once stayed with her family when she was a girl.

'He stayed with you, Oscar Wilde actually *stayed* with you?'

'I am afraid so.'

'Why have you never told me this before?' Even as I asked the question I realized that it was absurd. How *could* she speak of such a hideous happening?

The answer was characteristic. 'Because if I had known what he was, at the time, I should have run out of the house. I would have rather been in the room with a snake.'

But at last she brought herself to speak.

It was in the winter of 1883. Oscar had recently returned from a lecture tour in America where he had been exploited as a sort of brilliant clown. This was the heyday of his aesthetic period . . . the day of the velvet jacket, the flowing cloak and the soft felt hat. None of the major works had yet been written; the American dollars were soon spent, and on his return he was obliged to continue lecturing.

His first appearance was booked at the hideous, smoke-blackened centre of British industrialism . . . Leeds.

Now it so happened that on the outskirts of Leeds lived a formidable old lady called Rebecca Shalders, my grandmother. Although she was a model of Victorian propriety she was evidently keenly interested in the arts and whenever any celebrities arrived in the city she had a habit of annexing them. As she was hospitable, and not unintelligent, the celebrities were happy to be annexed. And they usually sang for their supper.

But Oscar did not sing for his supper. He was far too tired. ('Languid' was my mother's adjective.) Besides, he was extremely cold. The lecture-hall had been inadequately heated, the audience none too responsive, and afterwards there had been a five-mile drive through the snow in my grandmother's carriage.

So, after a large brandy and soda, he had excused himself, and made his way up the old oak staircase and taken himself to bed. He had made only one remark which my mother remembered. 'One's only real life,' he had said, 'is the life one never leads.'

'Never mind,' said my grandmother when he had gone. 'At least we will see that the poor man has a good breakfast.'

On the following morning my mother came down early to the dining-room to find the old lady hovering round the solid mahogany sideboard. This was laden with a weight of food which even in Victorian Yorkshire might have been regarded as almost ostentatious. Here my mother's recollection becomes crystal clear, maybe because she was later to inherit most of the silver plates and dishes in which it was served. Thus she vividly recalled the chafing dish filled with Grandmother's special kedgeree, the Georgian platters piled with sliced ham, the Regency sauce-boat with the pickled cranberries, the Sheffield plate which accommodated the cold grouse, and the cumbersome Victorian device, mounted over a spirit lamp, for the eggs, the bacon, and the sausages. At various times in my life I too have been served from the same dishes. But not all at once.

Oscar was very late. More butter had to be spread on the kedgeree and there was a fear that the spirit lamp might run dry. But at last he made his appearance. He was still wearing his fur coat, and my mother, with a curious flicker of memory (I was a tireless cross-examiner!), recalled that the collar was still damp from the snow of the night before, and that she had thought that the fur must be dyed and not 'good'. And he looked paler and more languid than ever.

'And now, Mr Wilde,' said my grandmother, 'what would you like to begin with?'

Slowly he surveyed the sideboard, and a faint but perceptible shudder agitated his body, which even in those days was beginning to run to fat. For a moment he stood there in silence. Then he walked over to the window, and looked out on to the cheerless landscape. The standard roses were muffled in straw, and in the distance the lake was a sheet of sullen glass.

He spoke very softly.

'I should like,' he said, 'some raspberries.'

My grandmother felt that she could not have heard aright.

'I beg your pardon, Mr Wilde?'

He turned and smiled.

He spoke even more softly, as though, in this incongruous atmosphere, at this unpropitious hour, a prose poem were forming in his wilful brain.

'Some pale yellow raspberries,' he said.

And that is the end of the story.

'Story'? How can one make a story from a single word? That is a question I would not venture to answer. For it was not I who said the word, but Oscar. He had a way with words.

Put it in Your Diary

FRED BASON

WHEN I was in my early teens the then famous James Agate recommended me to keep a diary. 'Some day it may keep you,' he said. I have kept a diary now for over forty years. I began as a nobody, and am still a nobody; but I estimate that more than a million people have read the diaries that I have had published. James Agate was not far out.

In Paraguay there is an elderly coloured lady who was, with her five children, at one time on the verge of starvation; she sold waste paper which she got from dustbins in order to keep herself and her family alive. She lived in a shed in a shanty town on the outskirts of the capital. She taught herself to read and to write. She kept a diary on odd scraps of paper because she couldn't afford to buy even the cheapest paper to write on. Faithfully for years she kept the diary of her very dreary life. One day she met by chance a journalist who begged her to allow him to read her diary. She was very reluctant; it was private and sad. Eventually, after much pleading, the journalist was allowed to read it. After a little editing the diary was published, and within six months it sold over 90,000 copies. It was (and still is) the best-seller of Paraguay! The lady is now a celebrity and lives in a luxury flat.

When I'd been keeping a diary for a number of years Nicolas Bentley came and asked to see it. Like that of the Paraguayan lady it was written on all manner of scraps of paper; they filled a hat-box in which my father once kept a top hat. Nicolas Bentley took away the hat-box and within six weeks he had compiled *Fred Bason's Diary* from that curious mixture of recollections, reflections, and memories. The book sold two editions of 5,000 copies; each edition within six months. It is now a rare book, and I, who wrote it, don't even own a copy! My fourth published diary was edited and introduced by Noël Coward—the only book in the world that's introduced *and* edited by this master.

Alas, the whole four of my diaries have not sold as many

copies as the one by the lady in Paraguay. I have not moved into a luxury flat. I have been fifty-two years in the same slum area of London. But I do not envy my fellow diarist; and on the whole I've lived a very happy life—made all the happier because I've been a faithful diarist for over forty years.

Mark you, there are good diaries and bad diaries. Here's an example from what I consider to be a poor diary. It was written by an Irish schoolmaster named John Fitzgerald.

> The criminals arrived at the gallows at ten-past-five and they were cut down at six-thirty. It was a charming evening, dry, and the sun was shining, although there had been several showers in the morning. Johnny and I went to Shinnicks and saw the execution.

Not a word about the poor men who got executed, or why they were killed. Not a word about the crowds or even where or what was Shinnicks. Yet John Fitzgerald got this diary published.

One of the greatest faults of budding diarists is to devote far too much space to the weather or what they have eaten. It took me nearly three years to get out of this habit. 'Yesterday it rained. I had a pair of nice kippers for tea.' So what? Would it make a ha'porth of difference to anyone in after years if yesterday had been a fine day and I'd had an egg for my tea? The purpose of a diary is to preserve interesting experiences. Of course, the terrible winter of 1962 was a unique experience and should have been recorded. I remember writing that I had no water, no coal, and no gas, and one day I stayed in bed all day simply to avoid the weather. That's a little bit of history. The weather is an inevitable subject of conversation the world over, and there are few diaries that don't mention the weather at all; but good diarists only mention it when it's exceptional. Here's another example of a poor entry—from some other diary:

> Mrs Burgess died in childbirth to-day—and the wind is west-north-west—but the sun did shine most of the day—although it was a little chilly for the time of the year.

What we'd like is more about poor Mrs Burgess, and less about the blooming weather!

Apart from the good and the bad, there are genuine diaries

and fake diaries. The genuine diary is written up regularly each day and is not addressed to anyone but the diarist himself (or herself). That superb diarist Samuel Pepys did not address his diary to anyone. He had no immediate reader, and most of it was in a curious shorthand that only Pepys could really understand. The fake diary is compiled with publication in mind.

It is imperative that the genuine diarist has complete sincerity. That's the first essential of every diarist. With hand on heart I can say I've kept a truthful diary since I was fifteen. Wasn't it Dr Johnson who wrote 'No man is a hypocrite in his pleasure'? My diaries are my pleasures. The pure (or genuine) diary is like an intimate letter.

An unpublished diary sent to me by a *Saturday Book* reader some years ago contained this passage:

> Getting out of bed in the middle of the night in the pitch dark in order to pee, I stepped full on a large drawing-pin that went right into my big toe. I swore words that I didn't even know I had in me as I withdrew that pin from my toe. I was in such pain that I hopped right back into bed. Holding my toe, I went to sleep. I quite forgot to make water.

That comes from the pen of a real diarist. He was not writing for an audience, but in an odd simple way he made that unimportant experience very real and vivid—and amusing.

Now here is a passage in a diary written about 1850 by a lady:

> I went into market this day. I spent 12 shillings, 9 pence. I was badly robbed. Will not go back to Mr ——. He is a robber.

Surely if you had been writing this passage you would have told what you spent 12*s.* 9*d.* on, and why and how you got robbed—any good diarist would have done that. It's significant little details that make an episode like this come to life.

Boswell once said that a good diary is recording for the sake of recording, without any consideration whatsoever for utility. Anyone can compile a diary, and most people will get a great deal of genuine pleasure from a record of their lives—if only they keep Boswell in mind and do not expect some Sunday paper to offer them a fantastic sum for the privilege of printing the diary. I have recently advised the head porter of a famous

London hotel to keep a diary; it should be fascinating.

I have read upwards of 350 published diaries in my time, and found about sixty of them to be really good. I must confess that I avoid the journals and diaries of modern politicians and generals. For the most part they seem to be written with an eager eye on serial rights. I have even known some of these modern political and military journals to be 'ghost written' because the politicians didn't have the time and the generals didn't have the intelligence. A 'diary' that is written for you by someone else is a contradiction in terms.

A good diarist must to some degree be an egotist—and yet must not be *too* self-centred. Whilst he must be extremely interested in himself, he must also be extremely interested in other people as well. James Boswell was perhaps the best example of what I mean. Boswell was an egotist (no one can doubt it), but his journals provide a superb spectacle of life in his times—people, places, and, of course, sex.

The true diarist never has or needs to have a reason for keeping a diary—it's done almost by instinct. Jane Carlyle recommenced her journal after a short break by writing: 'I began quite promiscuously without any moral end in view but just as the Scotch professor drank whisky, *because I like it, and because it is cheap.*' What better reasons could one have?

I keep a very strict rule to write up my diary around 11 o'clock each night—just before I say my prayers and go me to bed. Some days, of course, are not written up as fully as others. The average day is written up in around eighty words . . . short, concise, and to the point. Don't elaborate; just get the bare facts down. For instance, on January 30, 1963, I put into my diary:

Plum Warner, the cricketer, died today. I never got his autograph. I have a nice book on Cricket by him (and T. Hearne) in spotless fine condition, pub. 1900, and although it's been on my For Sale list for 6 weeks, NO-one will give me 2/- for it . . . Cecil McGivern of Television is dead. When Norman Collins left BBC, Cecil took his place. He gave me just ONE job. Norman had got me 7 TV jobs. I will wear a black tie to-morrow for Cecil. I will wear a black tie for a week when Norman Collins tips the bucket. This has been a lovely day. From Bush House I broadcast to CANADA . . . for 5 minutes. I go to bed this night in a very thankful frame of mind. The W.C. has been frozen since Boxing Day and now even the chain is broken.

That's all I wanted to put on record. I hardly ever buy newspapers now. Had I bought one that day I might have put in a great deal about the breakdown of the Common Market and all that kind of thing. Would it have been of any value?

On my jaunts and journeys I note such things as the prices of items in one district as compared to another: these go down on odd scraps of paper. If from a bus I see a small street market I note it at once, and return to it as soon as I can—for I know more about London street markets than most men—and like to keep up to date. If I go to a first night—with my autograph album—I watch the stars go in, note who they are, and by the time we come out I have thought up some questions to ask them. If they answer my questions (and they usually do) I write down what they said.

A diarist should have the gift of being both spectator and actor. It is this power that makes Pepys and Boswell shine above all other diarists. Pepys the spectator was profoundly interested in Pepys the actor. In a Boswell diary I came on this passage: 'I should live no more than I can record, as one should not have more corn growing than one can get in. There is a waste of good if it is not preserved.'

But what odd and unimportant things are—in the long run—worth preserving! Take the diary entry, for instance, that I wrote yesterday. It mentioned a tape-recording I did for the Australian Broadcasting Commission; the wonderful collection of Boy's Bloods belonging to my old friend, that fine actor, Frank Pettingell; and another actor, James Mason, saying: 'Garbo isn't all that attractive. She often has colds and a red nose.' Quite interesting stuff, you might say. But the Editor of *The Saturday Book* tells me the bit that appeals to him is this:

I'd been looking at 'Tonight' on TV whilst my housekeeper washed up the tea things. She came into the room just as 'Tonight' finished and Michael Rennie came on in a Harry Lime adventure. 'Oh,' she said, 'Michael Rennie! I must go and tidy my hair.' I said she looked very nice as she was, and Michael Rennie couldn't see her anyway. 'But I couldn't *possibly* watch Michael with untidy hair,' she said, and out she went. By the time she came back, all spruced up, the programme was nearly over.

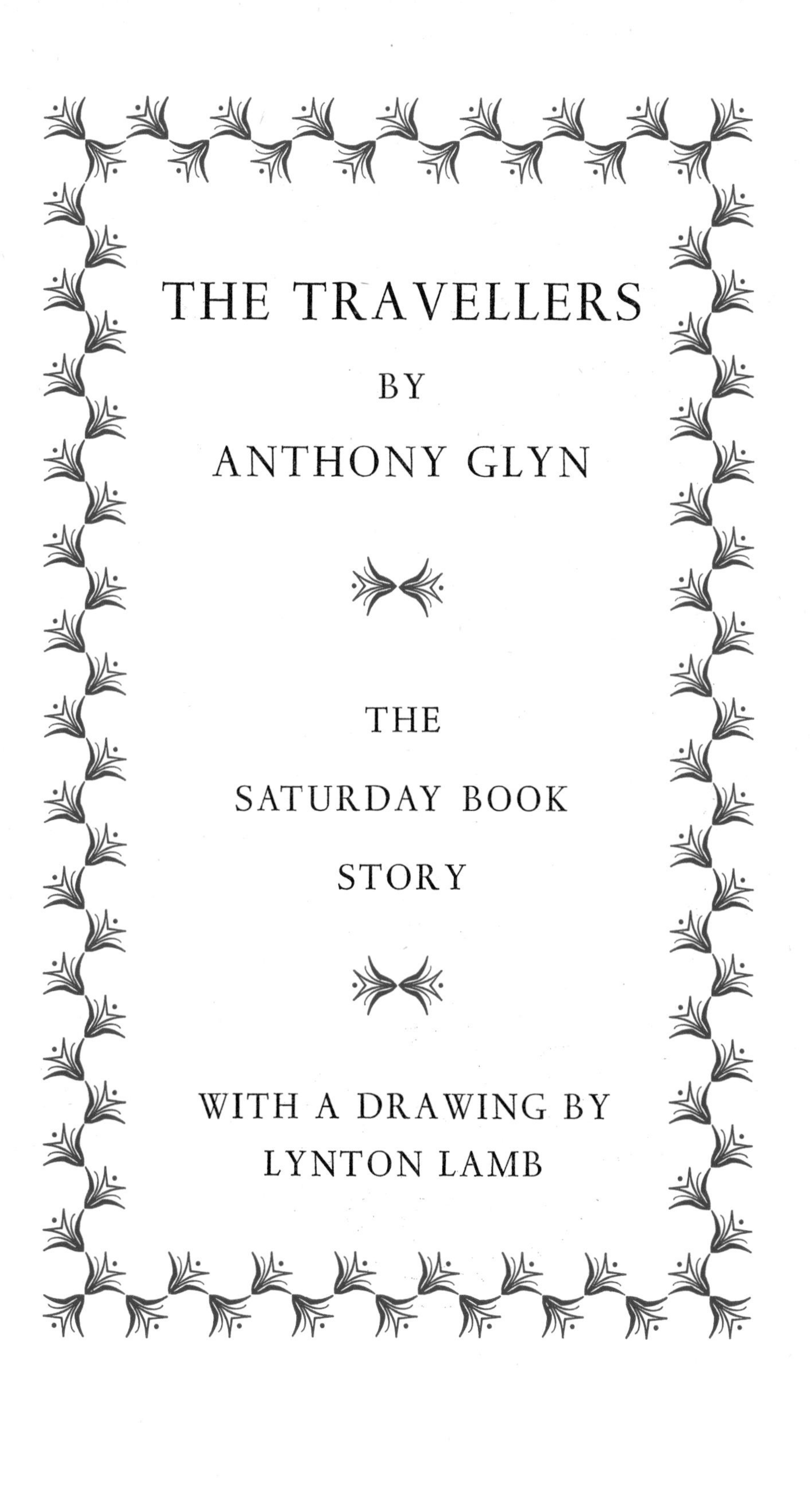

THE TRAVELLERS

BY

ANTHONY GLYN

THE

SATURDAY BOOK

STORY

WITH A DRAWING BY
LYNTON LAMB

WINGFIELD said: 'Draw the curtains, Peter.'

'But it isn't dark yet.'

'Draw the curtains and stop arguing.' Wingfield's voice was harsh, Peter's clear and high and unbroken. 'Do as I say.'

Peter went to the window, glanced briefly at the clump of fir trees beyond, and then pulled the heavy green curtains across. The room was lit only by the flames in the grate. He looked at his father, sitting beside the fire, card-tray on his knees, patience cards on the tray.

'And now switch on the lights.'

Wingfield said: 'Now come here. Stand there in front of me. Don't keep looking at that travel-brochure thing, look at me. Look into my eyes. I'm going to ask you something and you're going to answer me truthfully. Understand? Truthfully.'

There was a short deadly silence. Then Wingfield snapped it out. 'Where were you this afternoon?'

'This afternoon?' Peter was shrill with innocence. 'In here. Writing an essay. The one you told me to do. About the Andes.'

'You were not. You're lying.'

'I'm not, Father, I'm not!'

'I came in here and you weren't here.'

'Perhaps I'd slipped out for a moment.'

'You were gone sixteen minutes at least. Where did you go? I said, look into my eyes. Where did you go?'

Peter shuffled his feet and mumbled: 'I slipped out to get some chocolate.'

Wingfield's voice blazed suddenly. 'You went to the shop? By yourself?'

Peter's hands were damp. He gabbled: 'Well, I couldn't find Mrs Darwin and I didn't want to bother you when you were working, so I thought it wouldn't really—I mean, it wasn't for long.'

Wingfield stood up abruptly. The tray and the cards slid to the floor. 'Come and stand here. Here, right in front of me. Like that. Stand up properly, hands to your sides. Now we'll find out what's been going on. You say you wanted some chocolate, so you went to Mrs Brown's. You didn't tell anyone, you just went. Is that right?'

'Yes, Father.' A reluctant whisper.

Wingfield seized Peter by the shoulders and shook him hard. 'I will not have my orders disregarded. I will not have you slipping out of the house the moment my back is turned.' He pushed the boy away. His voice was ominously calm now. 'Now, Peter, why mustn't you go to the shop by yourself?'

Peter gazed at Wingfield, dazed, swaying. He answered in a dull, mechanical voice. 'Because I might meet people who would endanger me.'

'And how would they endanger you?'

'They would corrupt my integrity.'

'Why would they want to do that?'

'Because they would be jealous of my innocence.'

'How would they corrupt your integrity?'

'By suggesting to me insidious, half-baked thoughts.'

'Whom in particular do you have to beware of?'

'Girls.'

'Why do you have to beware of girls?'

'Because they would get me into their clutches and after that I should no longer be myself. I should be a slave to their vanity. I should have wasted my own personality.'

Wingfield relaxed. 'All right, you know it. You can sit down.'

Peter's legs gave way and he collapsed into a chair.

Wingfield said: 'Well, if you know it so well, why did you do it?'

'But, Father, I didn't see any girls. Besides I—I felt so cooped up in here. I just had to get a breath of air.'

'Cooped up? Breath of air? You've picked up those phrases from Mrs Darwin. I will not have you quoting Mrs Darwin's clichés. Which do you suppose knows better, Mrs Darwin or I?'

'You, Father.'

'And do you think I know better than you?'

'Yes, Father.'

'Then you will do what I say without arguing.'

'Yes, Father.' He sat quietly, hugging his knees. Then he remarked: 'But are all girls like that?'

'Yes, Peter. All girls. Scheming bitches. They just want to get you in their grasp to work for them. You leave this house, you find a girl, you marry her, and you'll never be yourself again. You'll never have time for a single interesting, imaginative, constructive thought.'

'But, Father.' The shrill note was coming back into his voice. 'My mother wasn't like that, was she?'

Wingfield began picking up the cards from the carpet.

Peter went on recklessly: 'I mean you married and you've had lots of constructive thoughts. You're still yourself.' Wingfield straightened the pack, tapping the edges on the tray. 'Father, do tell me about my mother. You've never told me anything about her. I've never even seen her photograph. What was she like?'

Wingfield stood up. 'Did you write me an essay?'

The keenness faded from Peter's voice. 'Well, yes, I did a bit of it, but I sort of——'

'You didn't do it! You went out somewhere else!'

Peter began to panic. 'No!'

Wingfield seized him by the shoulders. 'Yes, you went out somewhere else. There's something going on behind my back.'

'No, no, I didn't go anywhere. Only to the shop. I told you.' His voice squeaked with fear.

'I'll get the truth out of you. What were you doing?'

'Writing that essay on the Andes. And . . .'

'And what?'

'Well, nothing really.'

Wingfield shook him again. 'You'll tell me!'

Peter's voice was almost a scream. 'I did write my essay, I did. Most of it. But I wrote something else as well.'

Wingfield let him go at once. 'Show it to me. Go on, show it me.'

Peter stumbled to the table and picked up a piece of paper. He gave it reluctantly to his father. 'It's a poem.'

'A poem? Have you started writing poems, then?'

'Well, I don't expect it's very good. It, er, just sort of . . .'

Wingfield sat down again and started reading, frowning. Peter watched him, on tenterhooks.

'I don't expect it's any good really. I mean I'm not a great poet like you. It's only my first and I haven't——'

'Oh, shut up, boy!'

Wingfield took a long time reading it. Then he leant back and stared at the ceiling. Peter watched him in mingled dread and hope. After a while he couldn't bear it any longer.

'Is it any good?'

'It's almost very good.'

The sudden relief was overwhelming. He smiled exultantly. 'Oh, Father, if you say that, then it must be.'

'I said, it's almost very good. It's almost too good. It's wicked.'

The fear flooded back. 'Wicked? Why?'

Wingfield sat up and stared at him. 'Because it's stolen. It isn't your poem.'

'But it is. I wrote it!'

'The idea isn't yours, it's mine. I too wrote a poem called "The Silver Town". You couldn't even think up a new title. The idea's the same. Oh, you've made one or two alterations, every time for the worse. But this phrase, and that, and that—"A cone of glass shining in the air"—you've lifted that straight from my poem.'

'Oh, I didn't, I didn't!' Peter gabbled frantically. 'No, really, no, I'd no idea you'd written a poem like that too.'

'You've been into my study!'

'No, Father, no.'

'Slipped in against my express orders. You copied out my poem and made a few alterations, and then pretended it was your own. And showed it to me all smiling and pleased. Oh, how could I have a son like that!' He got up and stood over Peter.

'But, Father, I didn't. I was sitting here at the table. I knew I ought to be writing my essay, but this sort of came to me. I never read your poems, Father. I never went into your study.'

'And you never went to buy chocolate at Mrs Brown's?'

Peter looked up at him, pleading. 'Couldn't it be like this, Father? We're so alike, you've said it often. I'm your son. Couldn't the same idea have come to us both?'

'So it's hereditary, is it?'

'Or perhaps it's something you've said, talking about the Andes. But I never knew I was copying, really I didn't.'

Wingfield shrugged. 'I thought I'd seen everything that was strange in the world, and the strangest of all is in my own living-room. Still, I think one version of this poem is enough. We don't want to muddle the readers, do we?'

He put the poem carefully on the fire. Peter watched the flame, the writhing ash. He opened his mouth to say something, but nothing came.

'However, you have good taste. You chose a good poem.'

Peter asked unsteadily: 'Father, when can I read your poems?'

'When you're old enough to receive what they've got to give you. If you come to them too young they'll lose their impact.'

'But it does seem silly being the son of one of the greatest poets in the country and not knowing anything he wrote. Except one poem which I thought was mine and I got wrong even then. Father, couldn't you even read one to me? Or recite one? I'd love it.' Peter gazed at Wingfield, fascinated, devoted. 'I love it when you tell me about all the places you've been to, the Himalaya and the Andes and Mexico, Spain, America. The way you describe it. I know I'd love your poems too. Everyone admires you so much, and your poetry, and I don't know any of it.'

There was a long pause. Peter kneaded his fingers, his eyes pleaded. Wingfield slowly sat down again.

'All right, Peter, I'll say one to you. I'll try you out on one.' He leaned back and stared at the ceiling. ' "When I was but thirteen or so"—that's just like you, isn't it?'

'Oh yes, it is! Oh, go on, Father, do.'

'When I was but thirteen or so,
  I went into a golden land.
Chimborazo, Cotopaxi
  Took me by the hand.

I dimly heard the master's voice
  And boys far-off at play,
Chimborazo, Cotopaxi
  Had stolen me away.

I walked in a great golden dream
  To and fro from school—
Shining Popocatapetl
  The dusty streets——'

The spell broke. Mrs Darwin burst in.

'Excuse me, sir, but shall I lay tea in here or in the dining-room?'

'In here, as always,' Wingfield said with irritation. 'And later on at the proper time. We're working now. And leave the curtains alone, please.' Mrs Darwin was drawing them back.

'It's still broad daylight outside. It's a waste of the electric.'

'Leave the curtains drawn, please. The electricity bills are my business.'

'There'll just be nice time for Peter to get a breath of fresh air before tea. Go for a nice walk.'

'Any moron can go for a nice walk. Peter's got work to do.'

Mrs Darwin snorted and went out, banging the door.

'Oh, go on, Father, please go on.'

'No. No. She's spoilt it. She's broken the thread.'

'Oh, Father, please!' His voice quavered. '"Shining Popocatapetl, the dusty streets".'

'No, Peter. Not now. Well, did you understand it, what you heard of it?'

'Oh yes! It was wonderful. It was about me, wasn't it.'

Wingfield smiled. 'In a way. But you weren't born when I wrote that.'

'But that doesn't matter.' Peter squatted on the floor in front of his father, looking up at him. 'It's still about me, isn't it. Sort of foreshadowing me. "When I was but thirteen or so I went into a golden land." Oh, I loved it. It's all the mountains you're teaching me about. I'm so proud of you, Father. Is it your best poem?'

'Best? What's best?'

'I mean, is it your most famous poem?'

'I suppose so. It's the one people quote most often.'

'And you wrote it!' Peter glowed with admiration. 'Oh, please say the rest of it.'

Wingfield laughed. 'No. I've said enough for one day. Now what was that travel brochure you were talking about? Where are you planning for us to go?'

Peter leapt for the table and grabbed a shiny booklet.

'It's here. Only sixty-two pounds—guineas. Spain and Morocco. Seville, Marrakesh, and Tangier. Eighteen days, all travel by four-engined aircraft, hotels——'

'Seville.' Wingfield stared at the ceiling again. 'I'd like to show you Seville. The little white squares, the tunnel as you come through from the old Juderia and there is the spire of the Giralda. A silent finger pointing up into the dark blue sky, pointing to God, to Allah. And below it the great mass of the cathedral like an Arab kneeling down and doing obeisance. The orange trees in the courtyard, the dark little wine-cellars.' With each sentence his voice grew deeper, more musical. 'Where are we to go after that? Morocco?'

'Yes, we have five days in Seville and then on to——'

'Five days! Five years wouldn't be enough. What's the use of only five days?'

'But couldn't you show it to me in five days? I mean, you know it so well.'

'Yes, Peter, yes, I know it so well. I could show it to you in the twinkling of an eye. You hardly need to go.'

'I'd love to go. You did say we might go this year. I know I wasn't old enough to appreciate it all before, but you did say when I was thirteen. Why, it's like the boy in your poem, thirteen or so and went into a golden land.'

'You can go into a golden land in this room. I can bring it alive to you. I can make you see it all without having to fly about in four-engined aircraft.'

'Oh, Father!' he pleaded. 'Can't we go? You did say we might this year. The way you describe it all makes it sound so marvellous, I'm longing to go. Couldn't we go, Father, just this once?'

'Well, we may. We'll see.'

'Because I ought to write off and book us two seats. It says here, customers are advised to book early, as this will be a very popular tour.'

'Don't they always say that?'

'But supposing we did decide to go and then found it was booked up——'

'Then,' said Wingfield calmly, 'we should have to wait for another year. We have plenty of years ahead of us. Just as well, I have so much still to do, so much still to create. And so much to teach you, to make you see what it all means. Not what it means to tourists rushing through in their aeroplanes—five days indeed! But what it really means to a poet. I can do that here, in front of this fire. I can describe it to you so that you really will have been there. You will understand it more deeply and subtly than anyone on that tour of yours. Understand it with my spirit, see it with my eyes.'

'But it's not quite the same as actually going.'

'It's better. Better for you.' Wingfield rose, spreading his arms wide, embracing continents. 'Do we all have to see everything with our own eyes? Can't we take anything on trust? Can't we learn from anybody else? Do we all have to go back to the Garden of Eden and relive the whole of human experience? I have seen Seville, I have seen Morocco; you don't need to go. If you go and see them too you are wasting your time and mine. Learn from other people, Peter, learn from me, learn from your books. Lake Victoria Nyanza is in the middle of Africa. You can believe that, you don't have to go and make sure for yourself. I can tell you all about it. I have climbed in the Himalaya, I have climbed on Makalu, and so that is something you need not do. I have done it for you. I can give you that experience, enriched by my mind. Chimborazo, Cotopaxi, I have given them to you in my poem. You don't have to waste time and money in going yourself.'

Peter drooped, crestfallen. 'So we're not going. We're just going to sit here and talk.'

'Isn't that enough? If I were living in the middle of Africa people like you would travel thousands of miles to talk with me. But because I'm your father, in the same room, you want to rush away.' He crossed the room and picked up the heap of travel booklets from the table. 'All these brochures you keep sending for, glossy pictures, cheap journalese, I don't know why you waste stamps sending for them. I can tell you so much more. What was I telling you about this morning? Mexico?'

'Guatemala. You were telling me about Lake Ati——'

'Open your book, Peter, and take this down.'

Sullenly, sadly, Peter sat down and unscrewed his pen. Wingfield stood in front of the fire, staring at the ceiling.

'Lake Atitlan, yes. Take this down. It shines like beaten silver in the sun, and above it the sky is like brass and the sun is double the size it is anywhere else. It's a metallic landscape, the metal lake, the metal sky, the metal sun. And round the lake are little thatched villages, very primitive. Twelve villages, one for each of the Apostles. Their names ring like a carillon of iron bells. San Pedro, San Jaime, San Felipe, San Bartolomeo . . .'

Peter scribbled frantically, fighting back the tears.

Through the brassy glare of the Guatemalan day Mrs Darwin's voice came jerking. 'Tea-time!'

'Tea? Oh, is it?'

'Well, it's five o'clock, when your father ordered it.'

He came back reluctantly to the gloomy room. 'Oh. Would you like me to clear my books away?'

'Well, I can't lay tea with them on the table, can I?'

'No, of course not. Sorry.'

While he put his books away she pulled back the curtains and switched off the lights.

'Why, it's still daylight outside!' he exclaimed.

'Could be pitch dark all day long for all you'd notice in here. Cooped up with your books and things, it isn't healthy, a boy of your age. You ought to get out for a breath of fresh air in your lungs. Do you a world of good. Stop you looking so pasty-faced.' She started to lay the table. 'You ought to be at school, kicking a football about with boys of your own age. Running till you're red in the face.'

'My father says that sort of activity merely wastes time without any compensating advantages.'

'Hark at you! You ought to go to school and learn to talk ordinary like the rest of us. Can't think why the Cruelty Man hasn't been round asking questions. It's the law you've got to go to school nowadays.'

'An inspector did visit us a few years back but he was more than satisfied with my educational progress. My father knows so much more than any schoolmaster. Where would you find a teacher like him? My father says it isn't every boy that has the privilege of being given individual tuition by a poet of his stature.'

' "My father says, my father says." Can't you ever say anything for yourself? Anyway, it doesn't mean anything, all that what you've just said.'

'You don't understand, it's like being taught by Shakespeare. And, besides that, he's been everywhere, seen everything. Do you know he has climbed in the Himalaya? He climbed on Makalu, that's next door to Everest and nearly as high, and much more difficult. You have to be brave to do things like that.'

She snorted. 'Well, he wouldn't get far up Everest these days, would he. There! Well, now, will you run and tell your father tea's ready, because it's time I got the supper on.'

'But I can't. He's in his study.'

'Well, you can go and tell him, can't you?'

'No, I can't go in there when he's working. He's correcting the proofs of his new book.'

'Well, somebody's got to tell him, and it's either you or me.'

'He doesn't allow me to go into his study. He never has. I've never been in there. I can't go now.'

'Daft, I call it, a boy of your age. It doesn't seem right to me. Oh well, I'd better go and tell him, if you're afraid to go.' She stopped in the doorway. 'Well, I know somebody who's never going to be brave enough to climb Mount Everest, and he's not a hundred miles from where I'm standing now. Afraid to go to his father's study and say that tea's ready. Whatever next!'

She stumped out. Peter sat down and helped himself to jam. His face was crumpled and perplexed. He looked up quickly the moment she came back.

'What did he say?'

'He just said thank you he was coming. What d'you expect him to say? Polite as anything, too. And another thing, what's a writer like him with his books and his study and all doing on Everest anyway? Doesn't seem right.'

Peter said vehemently: 'Of course it's right! Poets aren't people who stay indoors all the time, too fragile and insensitive to go out and do things. They're men of action, men of adventure, they always have been. Look at Sir Philip Sidney, Sir Walter Raleigh. Look at Rupert Brooke and Julian Grenfell. Explorer-poets, warrior-poets, mountaineer-poets. Oh, I know my father doesn't do all that now, but he has done it all, my word he has! That's what makes him such a great poet, one of the things. That's why I'm so lucky being able to live with him and work with him and get to know him. It's an adventure in itself.'

'How you do talk!' She turned round and saw Wingfield standing in the doorway. Courteously he held the door open while she went out.

'Father, what was it like on Makalu?'

Wingfield put down his cup and looked at the ceiling. 'What was it like? It was a climacteric. It was a seminal experience. I think all my best poetry has been written about adventure, travel. Mountains especially. My Himalayan sequences.'

'Oh, I'd love to read——' Peter checked himself. 'Were you afraid at all on Makalu?'

'Afraid?' He smiled. 'Yes, I was afraid. That's one of the things you go to a mountain for—to know fear. A mountaineer without fear is like a mountain without ice, incomplete, maimed. But it's a different fear, just as it's a different ice. Some fears drag you down, lower you, diminish you. But mountain fear lifts you up, enlarges you. You go to the mountains to know that fear and live with it and come to terms with it—together with the joy and the triumph and the effort and the exhaustion. Fear is part of life, you must know it like everything else.'

'But you went on just the same. I mean, you didn't——'

'Of course I went on. You can't stop when you're on the rope.'

'No, of course not. What was the most frightening part? Where were you most afraid?'

'I knew fear most closely on the ice-ridge of Makalu. That was like climbing a frozen flame made of diamond, hard and glinting and leaping up into the air ahead of you. And dropping away underneath you into space. One slip and we wouldn't have stopped for five thousand feet.'

'But weren't you wearing crampons?'

'Oh yes, but they don't protect you from everything, you know, not on ice as hard as that. But at the time I don't think I'd have minded falling. I was in love with the air round me, the blue cold air, I was in love with the ice—and I was in love with my fear. Yes, Peter, I loved it. It was part of me, it was part of the mountain too, and it was part of that great day and that great place. That was one of the things I'd gone to the Himalaya to find, the love of fear. And that was what I brought back.'

'But you didn't quite get to the top, did you?'

'No, the monsoon broke while we were still at Camp Five. But did that really matter? I brought back something more valuable than the summit of Makalu.'

'Yes. Your poems.'

'I mean the knowledge of the love of fear.'

'I'd like to go there some day.'

'No, Peter, there's no need for you to go too. It's like Spain and Morocco, I've been there for you.'

'I don't mean just to see. I'd like to climb that ice flame too and find that sort of fear and conquer it.'

'You don't conquer fear, any more than you conquer a mountain. You live with it, you cherish it, you admire it, you learn from it. And I can teach you all that here in this room without your having to go to the Himalaya too. By the time I've finished with you it'll be just as if you had gone.'

Peter's enthusiasm died away. 'Yes, Father.'

'You think about that tonight when you're lying in bed, waiting to go to sleep. Think about the ice-ridge and the frozen flame of diamond, and in the morning you'll know all about it.'

By three in the morning Peter had been sitting on the little hard chair in his bedroom for over five hours. He sat in the dark, only turning on his torch occasionally to look at the time. He was cold and stiff, though he was fully dressed and had risen and stretched himself every fifteen minutes. He hadn't dared lie down on the bed in case he fell asleep.

It was two hours since he had listened, palpitating, to his father listening at his door. It should be all right now. He took the torch, softly opened the door, and slid out. In his socks he tiptoed along the passage, shielding the torch with his fingers. It took him five minutes to pass his father's door, trembling, hardly breathing. Then on, down the stairs, trying each step, before he put his weight on it. In the hall, before the study door, he paused. He took a breath, closed his eyes, and went in.

When he opened his eyes his torch was shining on a card-table covered with a partly done jigsaw puzzle. A sailing ship, it seemed. Puzzled, he went to the desk by the window, under the heavy green curtains. The desk was littered with newspapers folded open at the crossword puzzle. He shuffled among them cautiously, searching, finding nothing. Greatly daring, he sat down in his father's chair. On the blotter was the latest crossword puzzle. His heart thumped noisily in the dusty silence.

Gently he opened the desk drawers, and then shut them again. He flashed the beam round the room, baffled, irresolute. By the fireplace was a table with books on it. Perhaps they were there. He tiptoed to the table and looked at the books. They were all well-fingered thrillers, detective stories. No poems, no proofs. On the opposite wall was a bookcase. The top shelf had more thrillers, but the second shelf had guidebooks, travel books, mountaineering books. The third shelf had poetry.

Excitedly he dropped to his knees. Shakespeare, Milton,

Keats, Shelley, the Oxford books of verse. The beam of the torch moved along the shelf, searching for Wingfield's collected poems, Wingfield's Himalayan sequences, not finding them.

He squatted back on his heels, puzzled. Then an idea came to him. He pulled out the *Oxford Book of Modern Verse* and found the index of authors. Warner, Wellesley, Wilde, Yeats. No Wingfield.

Idly he turned the pages, the index of first lines. One of them caught his eye, and he jumped. 'When I was but thirteen or so.' He'd found it, it was here. Excitedly he flicked over the pages. There it was. 'I went into a golden land, Chimborazo, Cotopaxi took me by the hand. . . .' But his father's name was not there. The poem was called 'Romance' and it was by W. J. Turner.

He gazed at the name appalled. His heart echoed round the room.

Wingfield asked: 'Aren't there any letters for me this morning?' Frowning he drew the curtains across the dining-room windows.

Mrs Darwin said: 'Only just those for Peter. He gets more letters a day than you get in the whole year.'

'Nonsense they all are. Travel brochures, advertisements, free samples. The Scottish Tweed Association. I don't know why he bothers to send for that stuff. Where is he, anyway?'

'He's late. Must have fallen asleep after I called him.'

Mrs Darwin went out. Wingfield leafed through the letters on Peter's plate again with irritation, and then sat down and helped himself to cornflakes. A minute later Peter burst in, tousled and breathless.

'You're late.'

'Sorry, Father. I overslept.'

'And look here, I'm going to stop you sending for all this rubbish. There's no point in it.'

'They're for me?' Peter said brightly. 'Oh, what a lot! I love getting letters, thinking that someone outside knows about me and wants to write to me.'

'Even if it's only a catalogue for tweeds?'

Peter smiled, and then suddenly stopped smiling. He reached for the cornflakes, and then withdrew his hand.

'Father, I got up in the night.' He spoke in an unusually low voice. 'I came downstairs and went into your study.'

'You what! You went into my study? But you *know*——'

Peter went on steadily: 'I had to go in there. It was like the ice-ridge of Makalu. I was afraid to go in and so I had to go.'

Wingfield blazed at him: 'You disobedient little twister. The moment my back is turned, the moment I'm asleep—You'll regret this.'

'I had to go. The ice-ridge was a frozen flame made of diamond and you lived with your fear till you loved it. I had to go too. It was my ice-ridge.'

'Well, was it worth it? Was it very exciting in there?'

'Yes, it was, it was.' Peter helped himself calmly to cornflakes.

Wingfield lost patience. 'Well, what did you find there, besides fear?'

'Jigsaw puzzles, crossword puzzles, detective stories. I didn't find your proofs, your new book.'

'You wouldn't have. I took them up with me to bed.'

'And I looked in the bookcase for your poems, your Himalayan sequences. But I couldn't find them either.'

'Of course not. They're in my bedroom too.'

'You said you kept them in your study.'

'So I do. But I took them upstairs last night. Perhaps I had an inkling that someone might come prowling round in the night.'

'I wanted to read them, make sure I didn't copy any more of them by mistake. I looked in the *Oxford Book of Modern Verse* in case they might be there.'

Wingfield said easily: 'Oh, you won't find any there. I'm still too young for that. Though I may be in the next edition. They're discussing that now.'

'But I did find one there.' Peter's voice was still low. 'Your most famous poem. "When I was but thirteen or so".'

Wingfield put down his spoon, staring at Peter. 'Is that in there? Oh yes, so it is! I remember now, I'd forgotten.'

'But it isn't by you. It's by someone called W. J. Turner.'

Wingfield looked at the ceiling and laughed. 'Oh, think you've caught me out, do you? W. J. Turner. Yes, how that takes me back. Want to know why I published that poem under the name W. J. Turner?' Peter said nothing, and Wingfield went on: 'I wrote the poem at Cambridge. I'd just come back from South America, and I sent it in for a university prize. All the entries had to be under pseudonyms, and I just happened to choose the name W. J. Turner. It was the name of my butcher. I looked out of my window and saw his van in the street below. It was a dark green van, and it was all wet in the rain, and——'

'Father, did you really write that poem?' Peter's voice was a little louder.

'Of course I did. I've just told you. It won first prize.'

'Have you ever published any poems? Have you ever written any? Are you really a famous poet?'

'Well, really, what a thing to say to your father. Leave your breakfast, go to your room, now, this minute!'

'Have you really climbed in the Himalaya? Have you really been to Mexico and the Andes and Morocco and Spain?'

Peter looked at his father for the first time that morning. Their eyes met. There was a moment of silence.

Wingfield said at last: 'Yes, of course I've been to Spain.'

Peter suddenly began to cry. His face crumpled and tears ran down his cheeks. Wingfield heaved his chair round.

'Listen, Peter, I've got to tell you something. I hadn't meant to tell you yet, but you've forced me to. I don't know if you'll be able to understand, but you must try.'

Peter sobbed: 'You haven't been to any of them. You never climbed on Makalu, you never wrote any poetry. It's all a story.'

Wingfield said sharply: 'Look at that tea-cosy, Peter. What colour is it?'

'It was all lies all the time. Just lies.'

'Peter, will you listen to me! What colour is that tea-cosy? It's red, isn't it? You think it's red, don't you? So do I. So does Mrs Darwin. And so it is red. It's red to us, and so it's red altogether. But it isn't red, really. Colours are all illusion. There's no colour in that, it hasn't any colour. It isn't red in itself, it isn't red if you're colour-blind. It isn't red if you're a camera. But to us it seems to be red and so it is red. Do you see?'

Peter howled: 'My poem! The one you burnt because it was just like one of yours. But you hadn't written one. You just burnt it out of spite.'

'Well, it wasn't a very good poem. The fire was the best place for it. But listen, what seems to be, is. The sky seems to us to be blue. But if you go up and look at it in an aeroplane it isn't any colour. But it still seems to be blue to the people on the ground, and so it is blue. I seem to you to be a great poet, and so I am a great poet. I seem to be a great mountaineer, and so I am one. Do you understand?'

'You didn't have to tell me all those lies.'

'They weren't lies, can't you see? They were true, like the tea-cosy being red. That's true in the same way. Now listen, Peter, when you were a very small baby and your mother went away, and I realized I'd got to bring you up all by myself, I thought how can a man best bring up a son? What would be the finest training for you, the finest education? And I thought the finest thing would be to be brought up by a man, a great man, a man you could admire and look up to. A man of action, an explorer, a traveller, a mountaineer, a great poet, someone who had written something the world would not willingly let die. If you were to be brought up by such a man, with him all the time, seeing his mind, learning from him, living with him, seeing nobody else, only him—that would be the finest education any boy could have. So I gave it to you. Just like that. It didn't matter if I'd written any poetry or not, it didn't matter if I'd climbed on Makalu or not. All that mattered was that you should believe that I had. And then it would be true.'

'No! No! It's not true, it's a lie and you burnt my poem.'

'I was afraid you were still too young to understand.'

Peter screamed at him: 'Do you know what I'm going to do? I'm going to all those places you pretend you've been to. I'm going to them all myself, and I'm going to write poems about them. I'm going to be a great poet and I'm never, never, never coming back.'

He choked and slammed out of the room. Wingfield shook his head and went on with his breakfast. When Mrs Darwin came in he said: 'You can clear away now. Peter has finished too.'

'I just seen him run by the kitchen window. Oh, he hasn't touched a thing. Didn't he want it?'

'He hadn't got much appetite this morning. I think he had rather a disturbed night. I sent him out to get a breath of fresh air before we start work.'

'Well, that's a nice change. Do him good. He looked to me as if he was going somewhere in a hurry.'

'Oh, he hasn't gone far. He'll be back quite soon. He's got nowhere else to go.'